KING GABE'S WORLD

THE BEST OF KING GABE'S ARTWORK

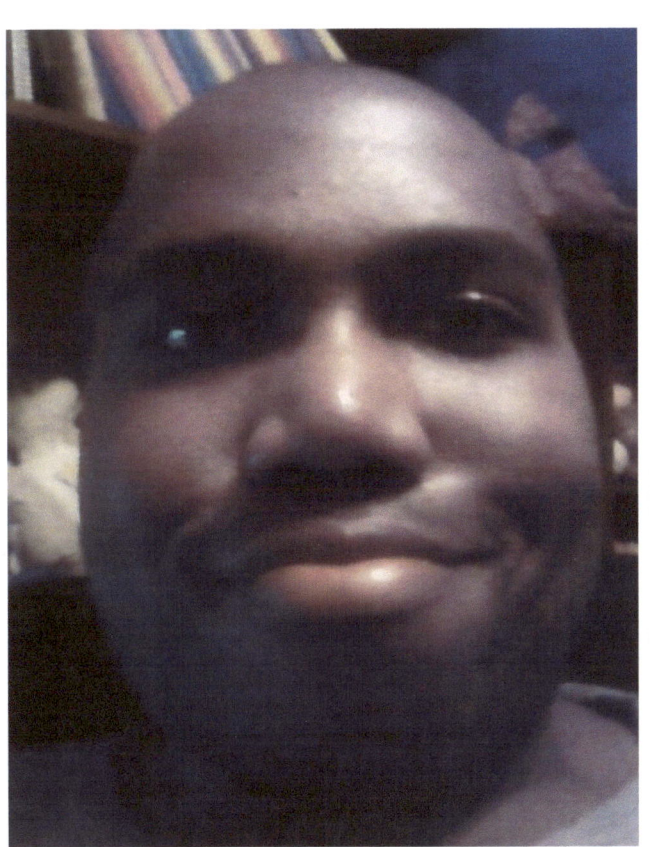 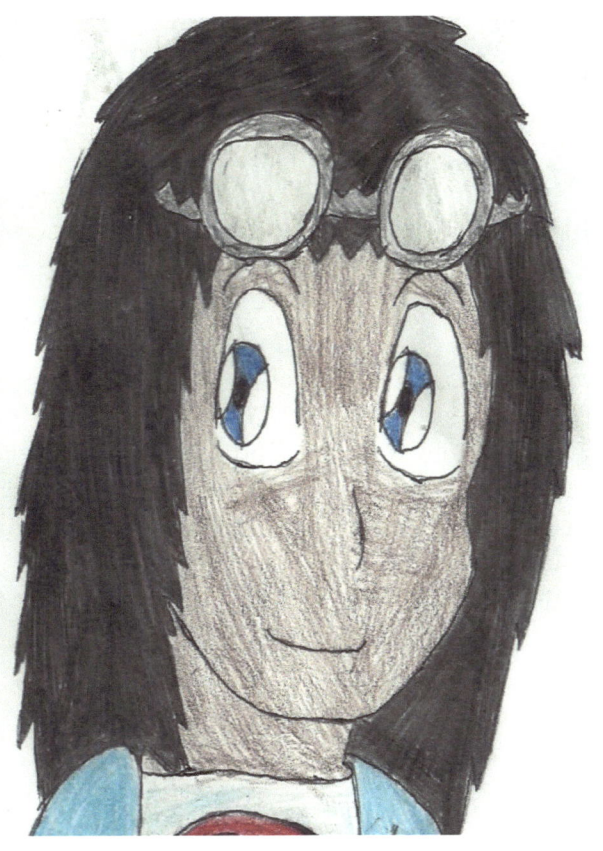

BY: GABRIEL "KING GABE" JOHNSON

This is a work of fiction. The events and characters described herein are imaginary and are not intended to refer to specific places or living persons. The opinions expressed in this manuscript are solely the opinions of the author and do not represent the opinions or thoughts of the publisher. The author has represented and warranted full ownership and/or legal right to publish all the materials in this book.

KING GABE'S WORLD
THE ARTWORK OF KING GABE
All Rights Reserved
Copyright © 2012 Gabriel "King Gabe" Johnson
v1.0

Cover artwork and images © 2012 Gabriel "King Gabe" Johnson

This book may not be reproduced, transmitted, or stored in whole or in part by any means, including graphic, electronic, or mechanical without the express written consent of the publisher except in the case of brief quotations embodied in critical articles and reviews.

PRINTED IN THE UNITED STATES OF AMERICA

This is an epic battle: God, Super A, Super B, Super G, and Super E versus the Devil, Super D, Super O, and Super F.

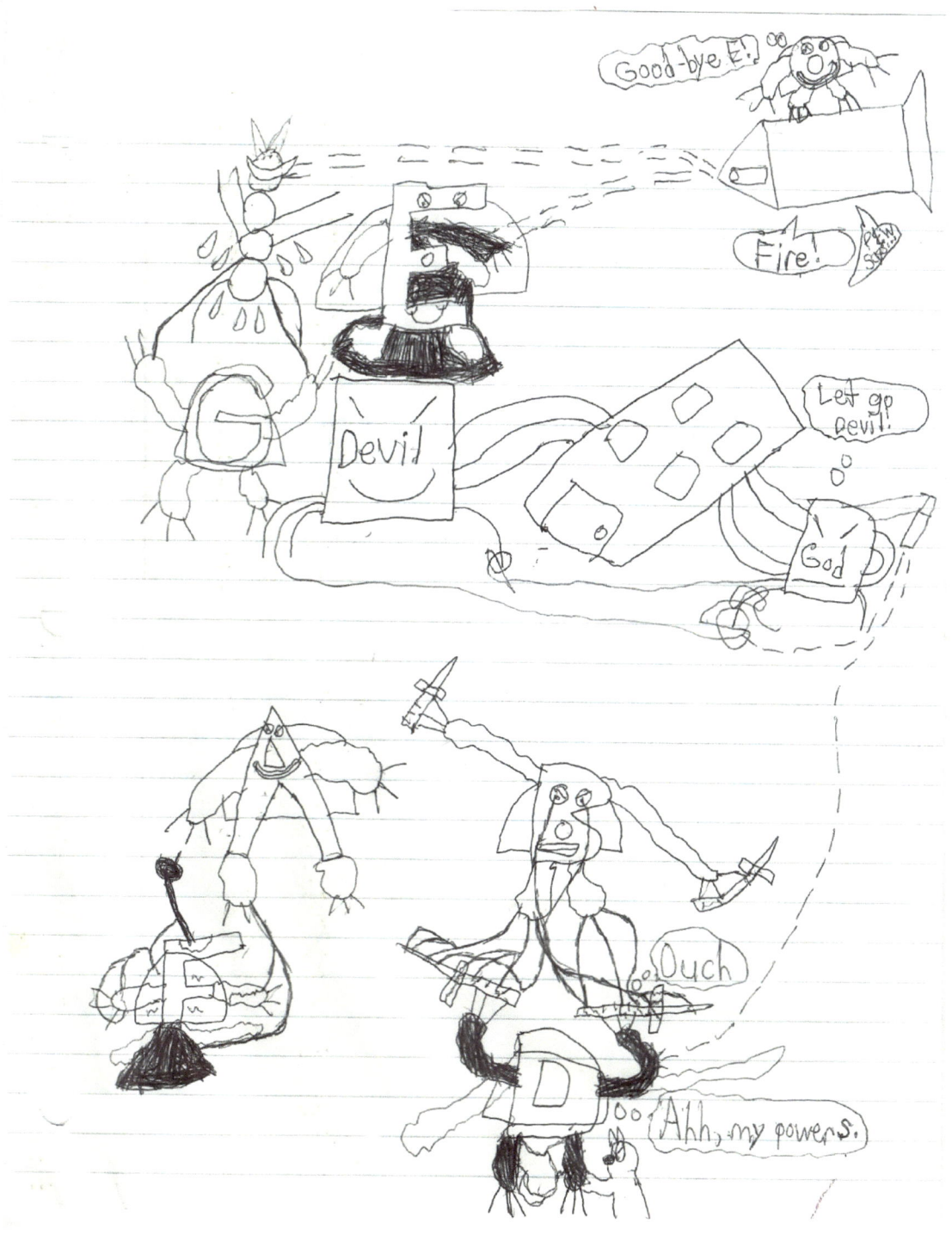

GABE, LOOKING COOL, WHILE SITTING ON HIS GRANNY'S PORCH IN 1995

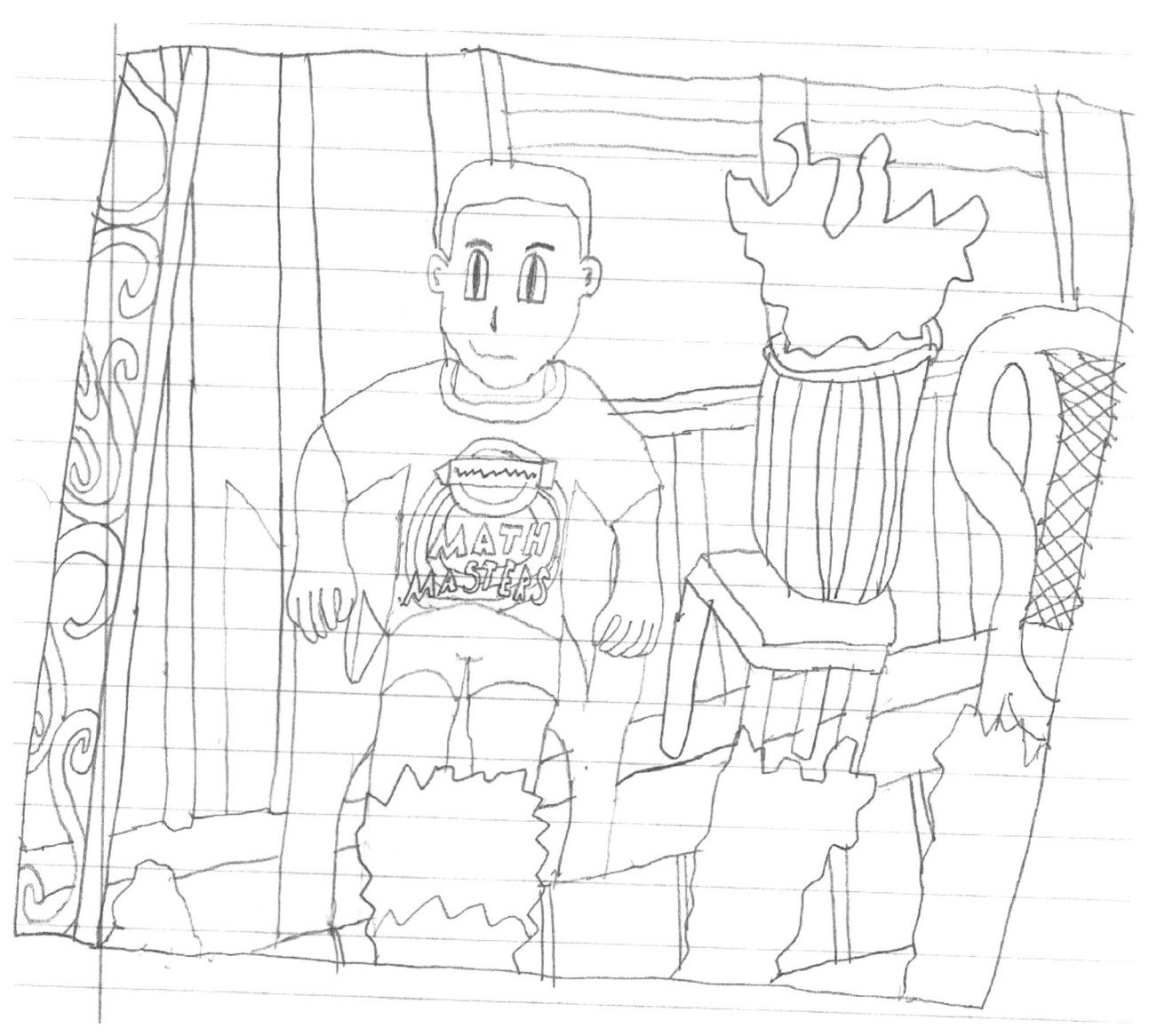

GABE'S BIG PAPA DOING A LITTLE WEIGHT LIFTING

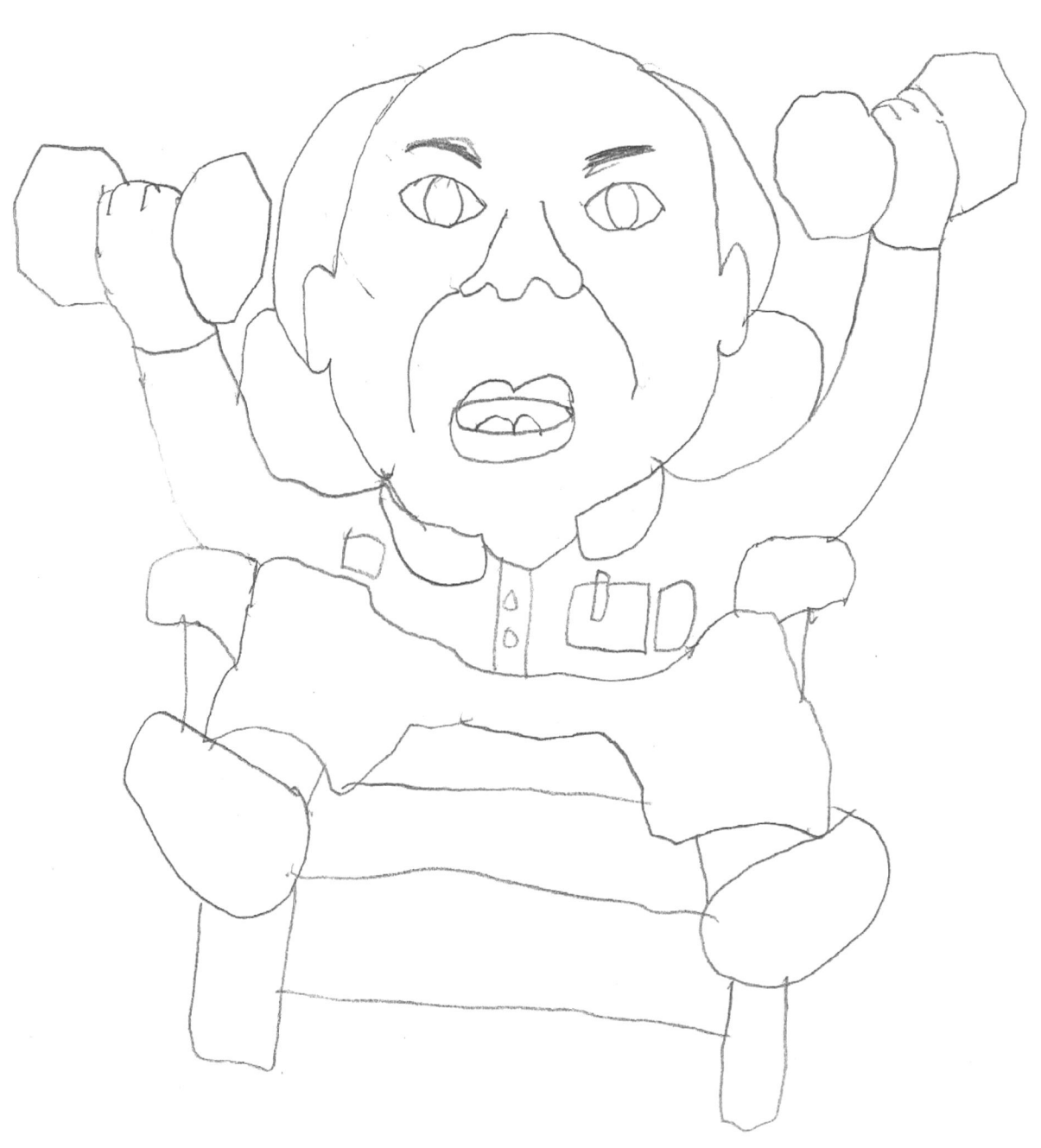

GABE'S IMAGINARY HAMSTER, BLUE

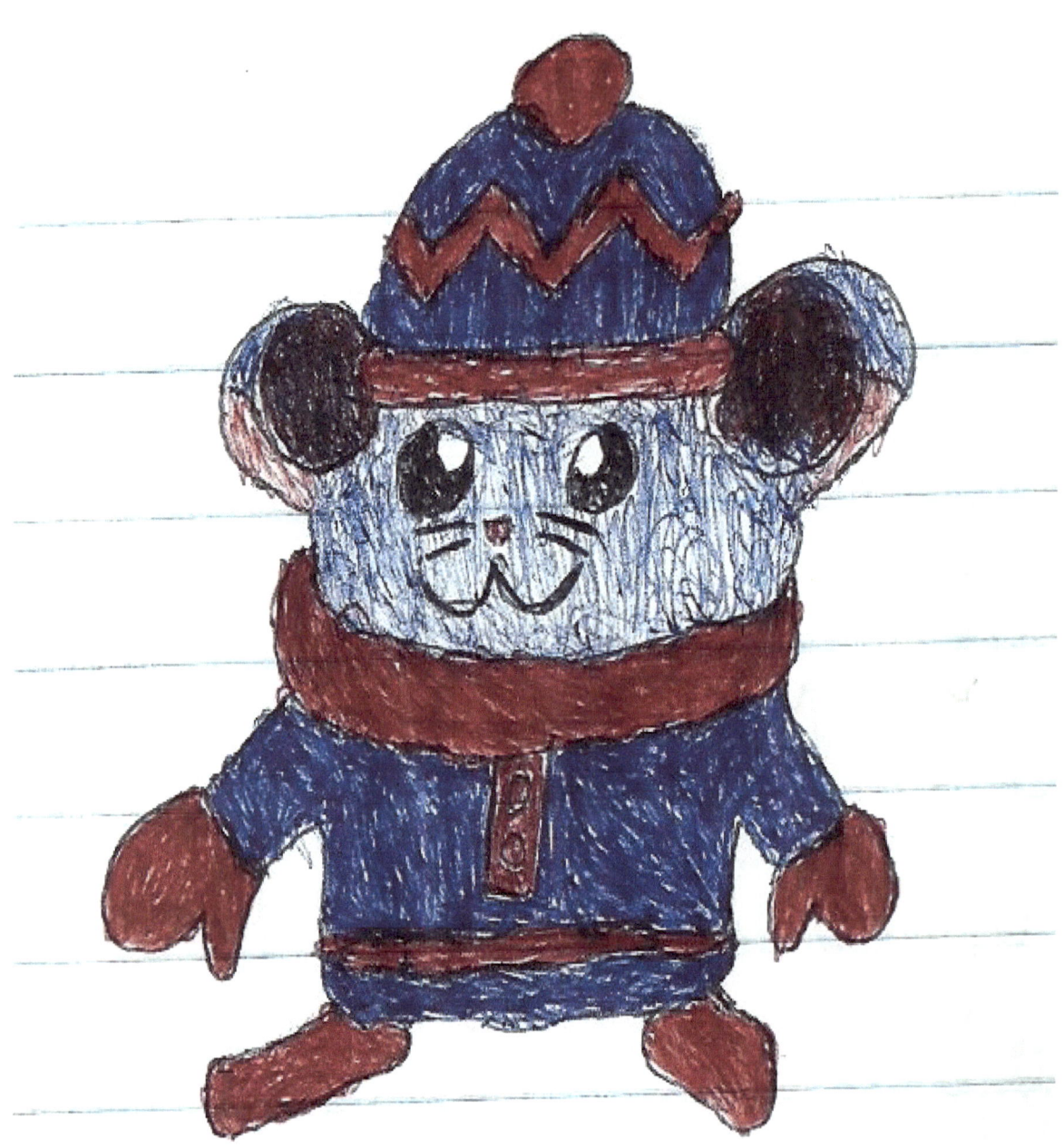

STAR STRIKER

FROM 2004 IN RED AND BLUE WITH 3D GLASSES

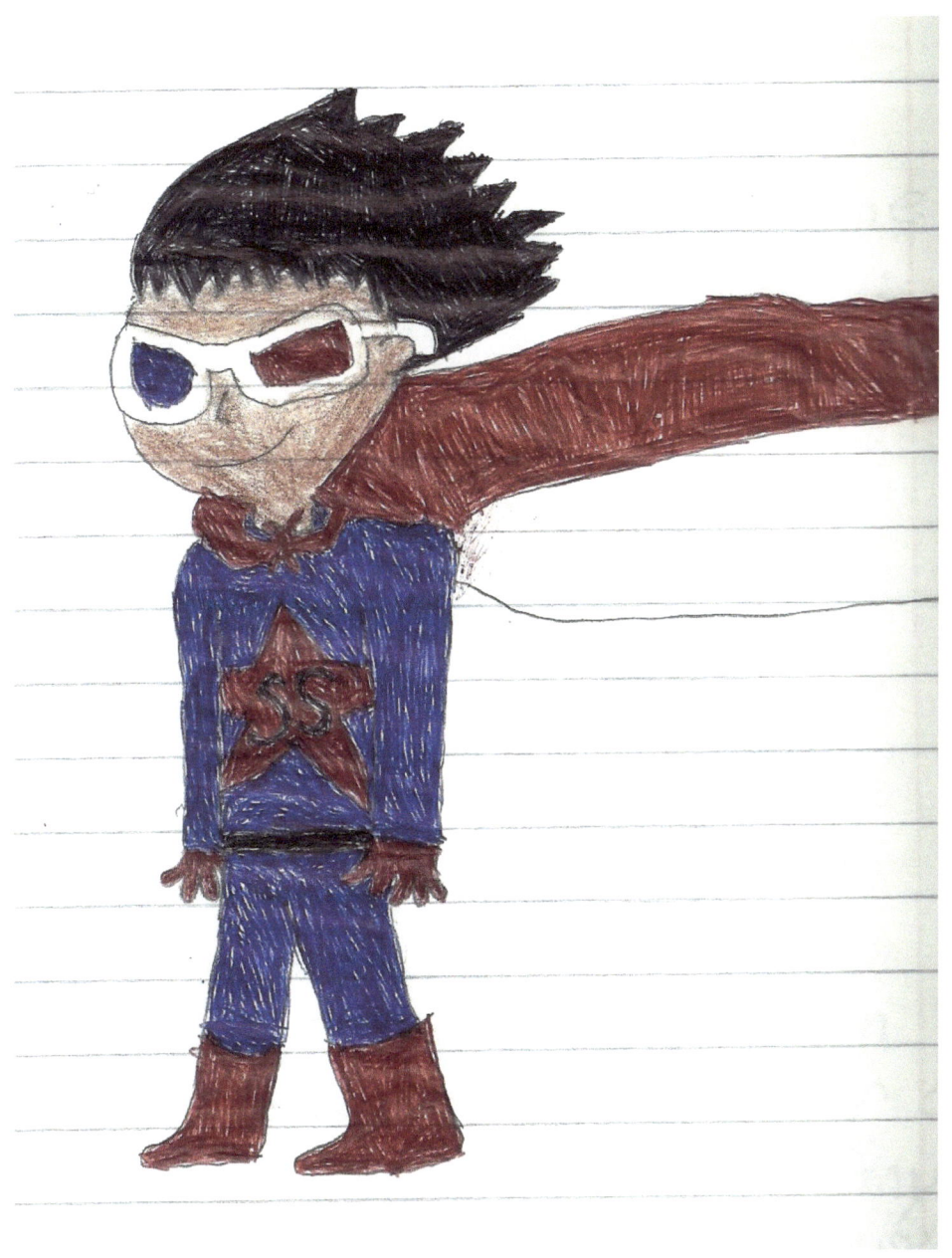

THE DREAM LEAGUE 2004 VERSION

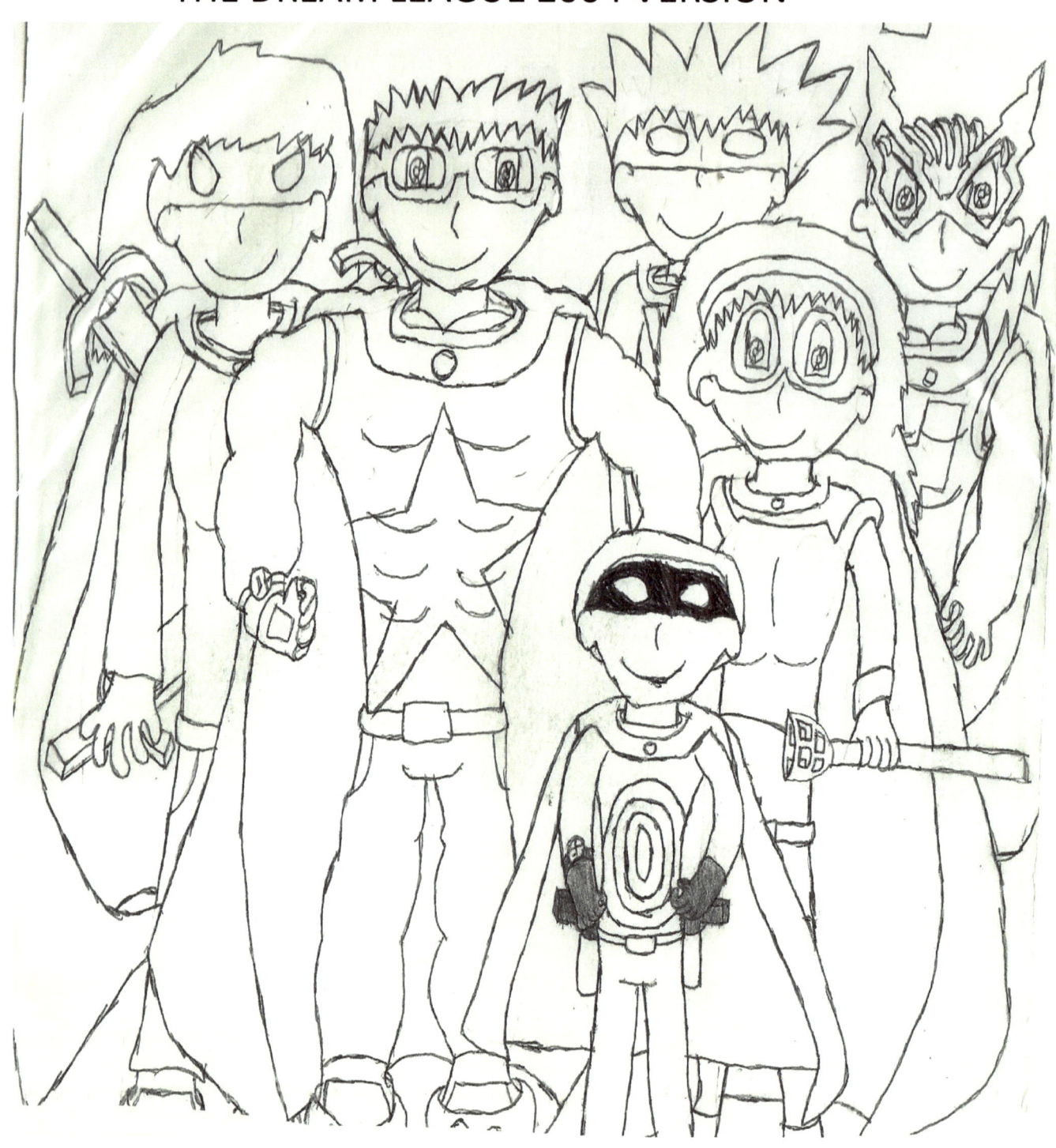

BERA THE TEENAGE WARRIOR

HALF HUMAN, HALF FOX

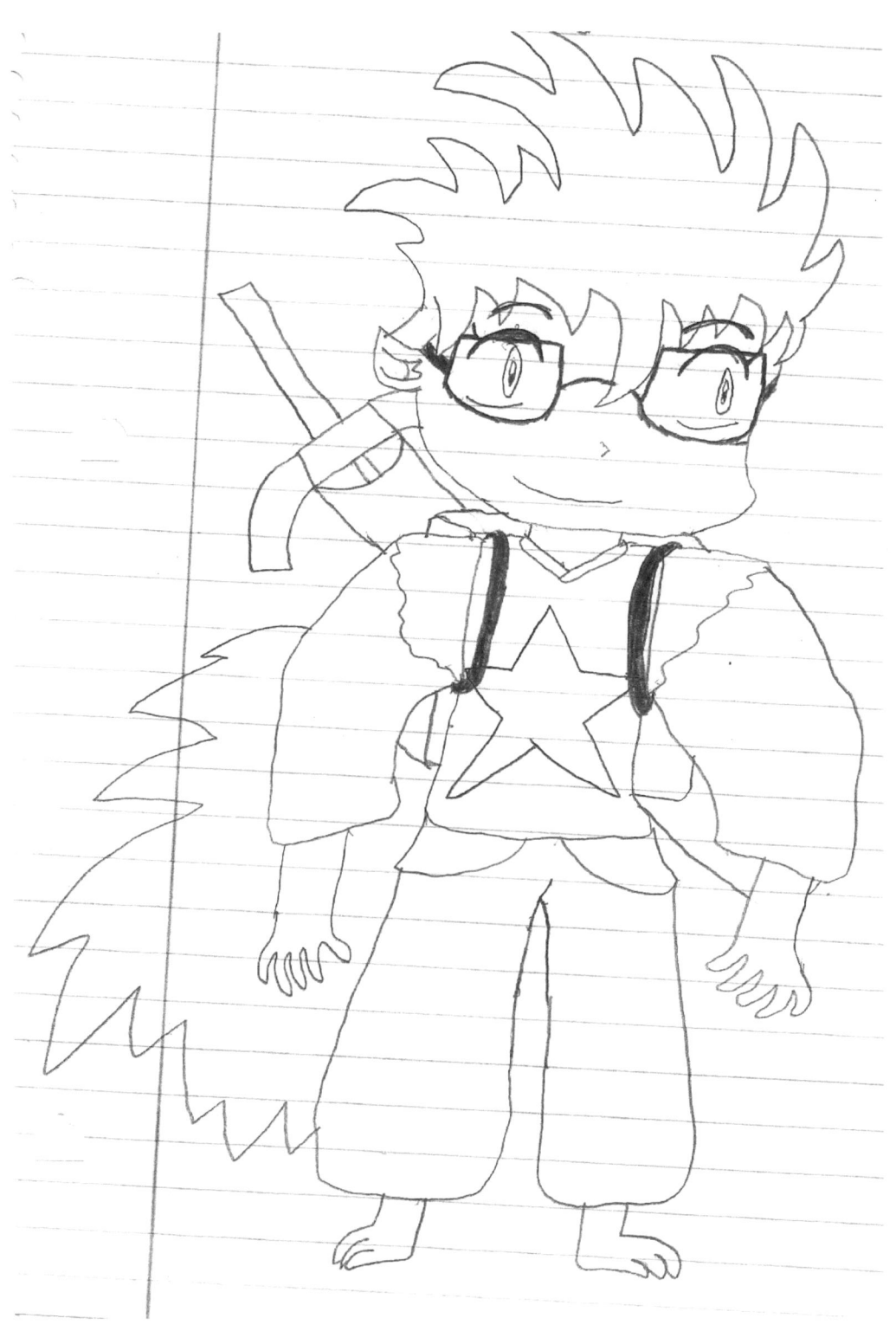

THE MIGHTY VASUKI DRAGON: VERSION ONE

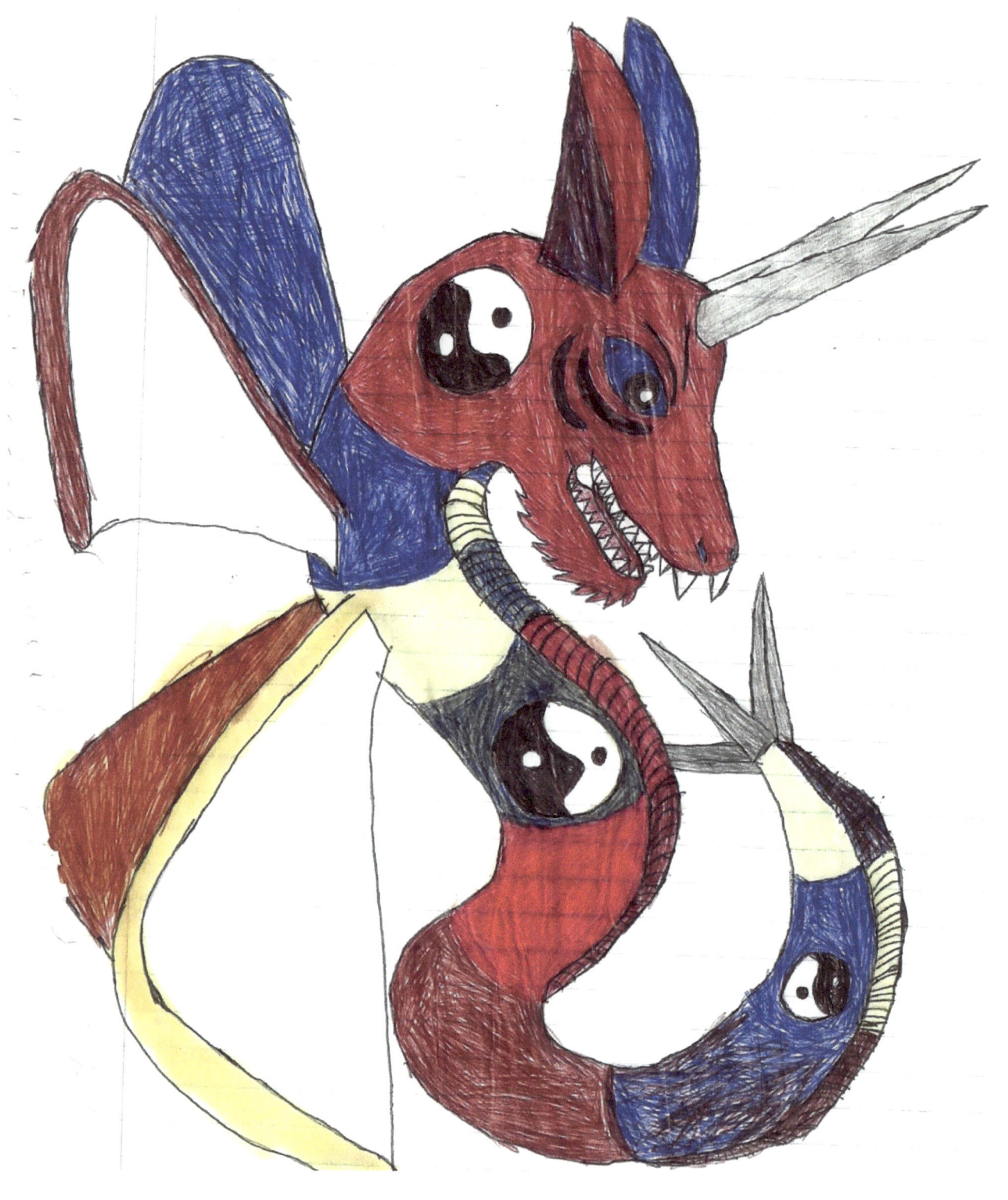

GABE'S IMAGINARY BROTHER: DARIUS

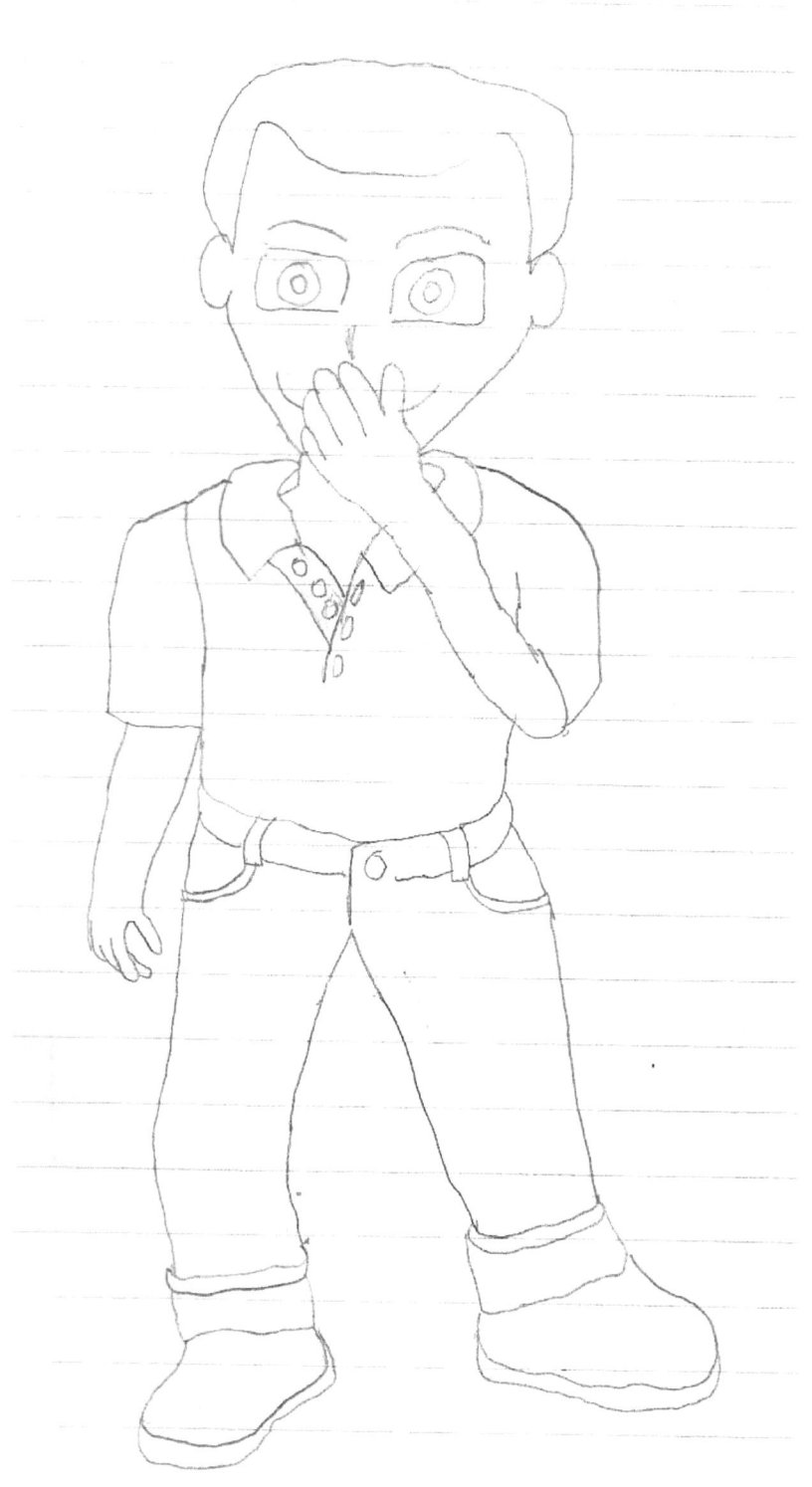

THE PHANTOM MOON BLADER

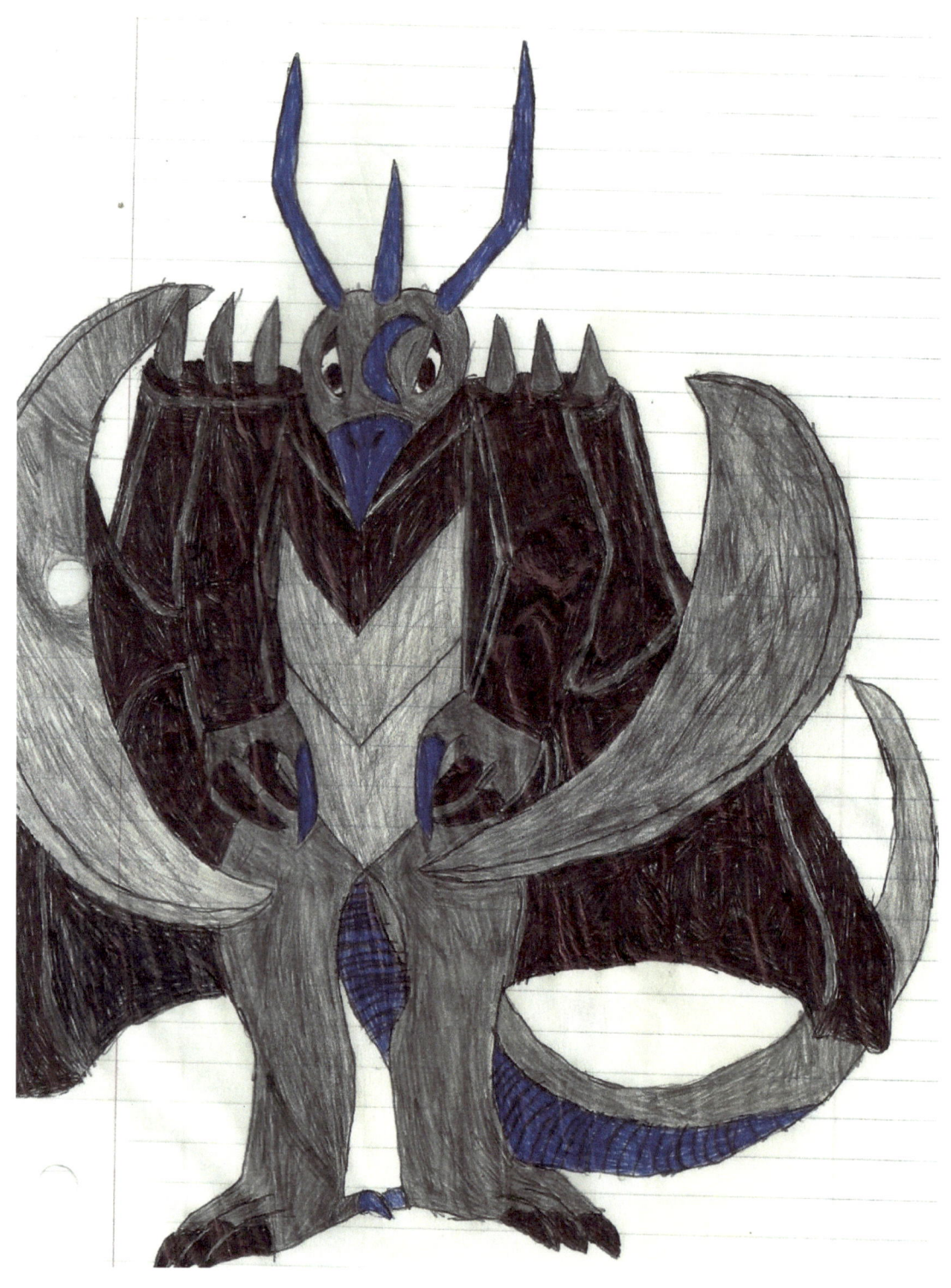

THE MIGHTY VASUKI DRAGON: VERSION TWO

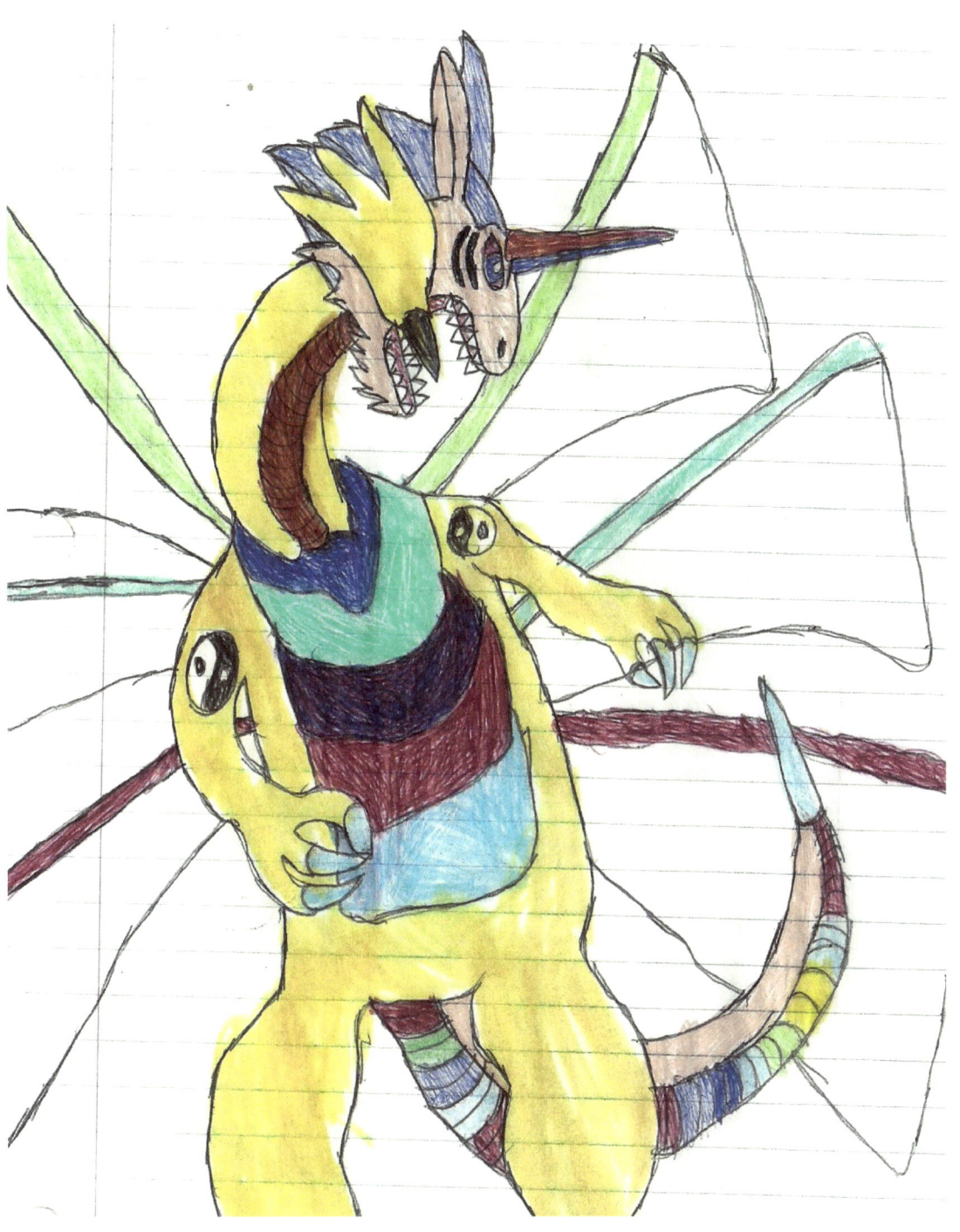

GABE'S IMAGINARY SISTER, TIYANA (A.K.A. TIKARI):

VERSION ONE

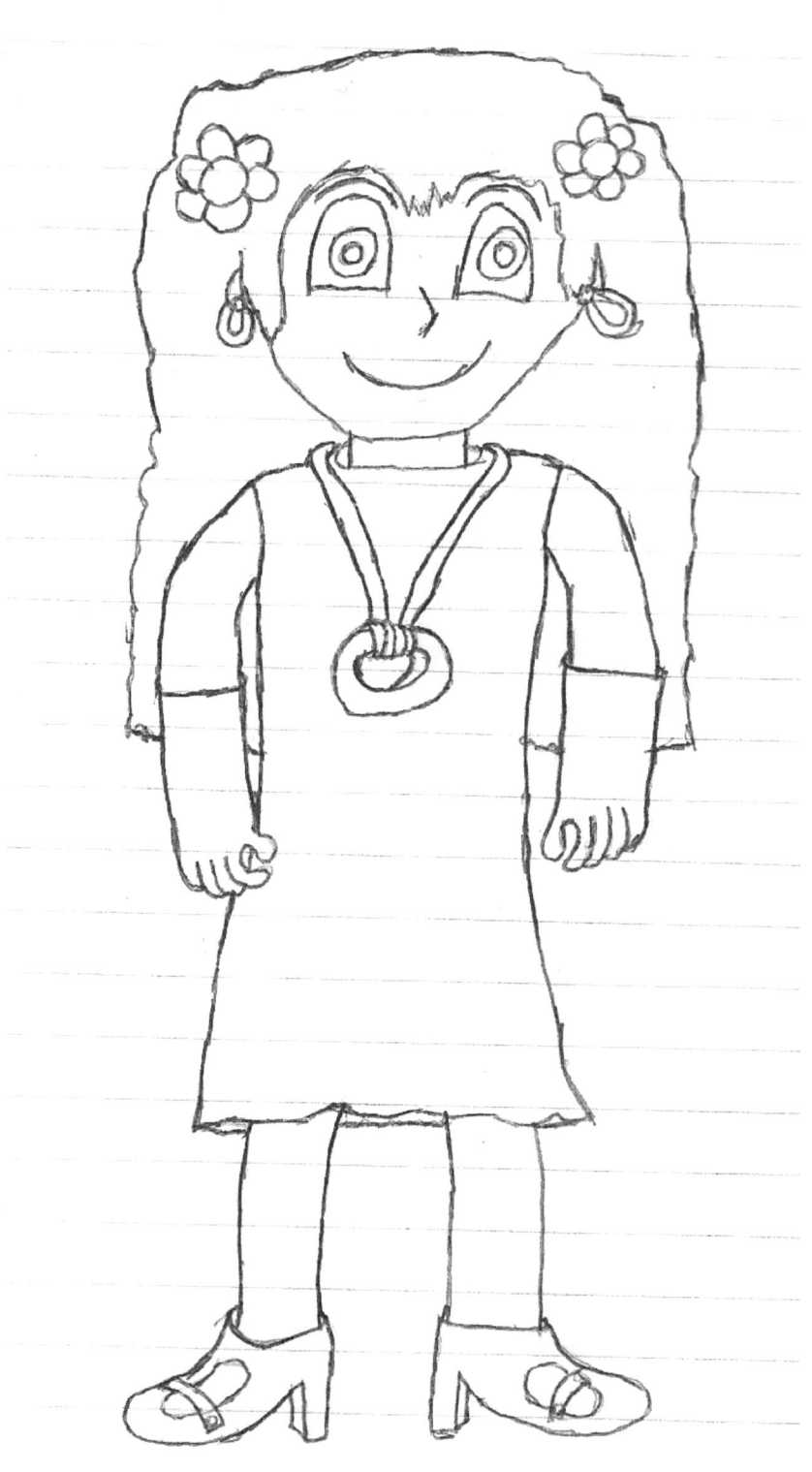

KIDS OF THE FUTURE FANTASY FROM HIGH SCHOOL

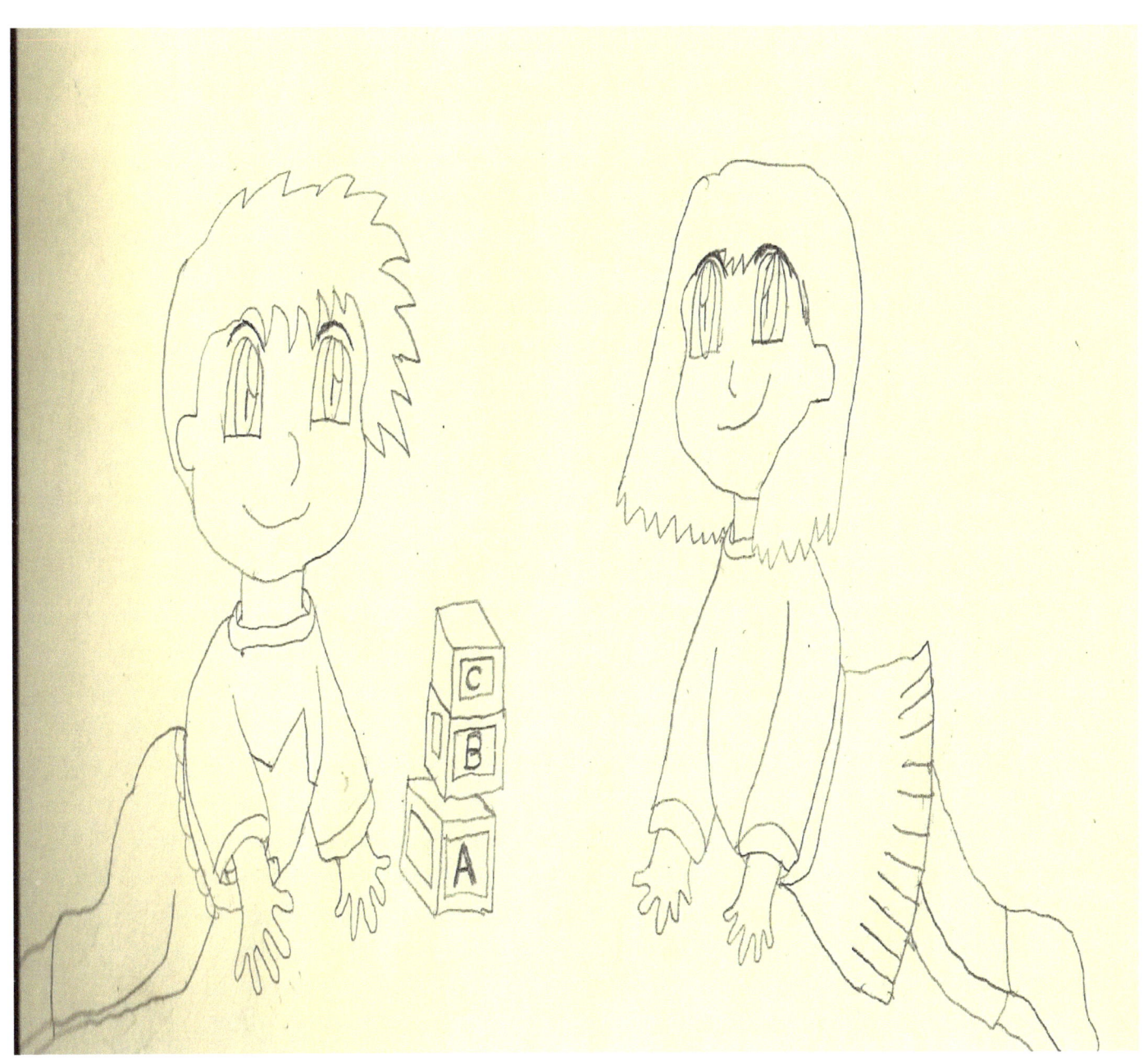

A MYSTERY ANIMATED PAGNENT QUEEN

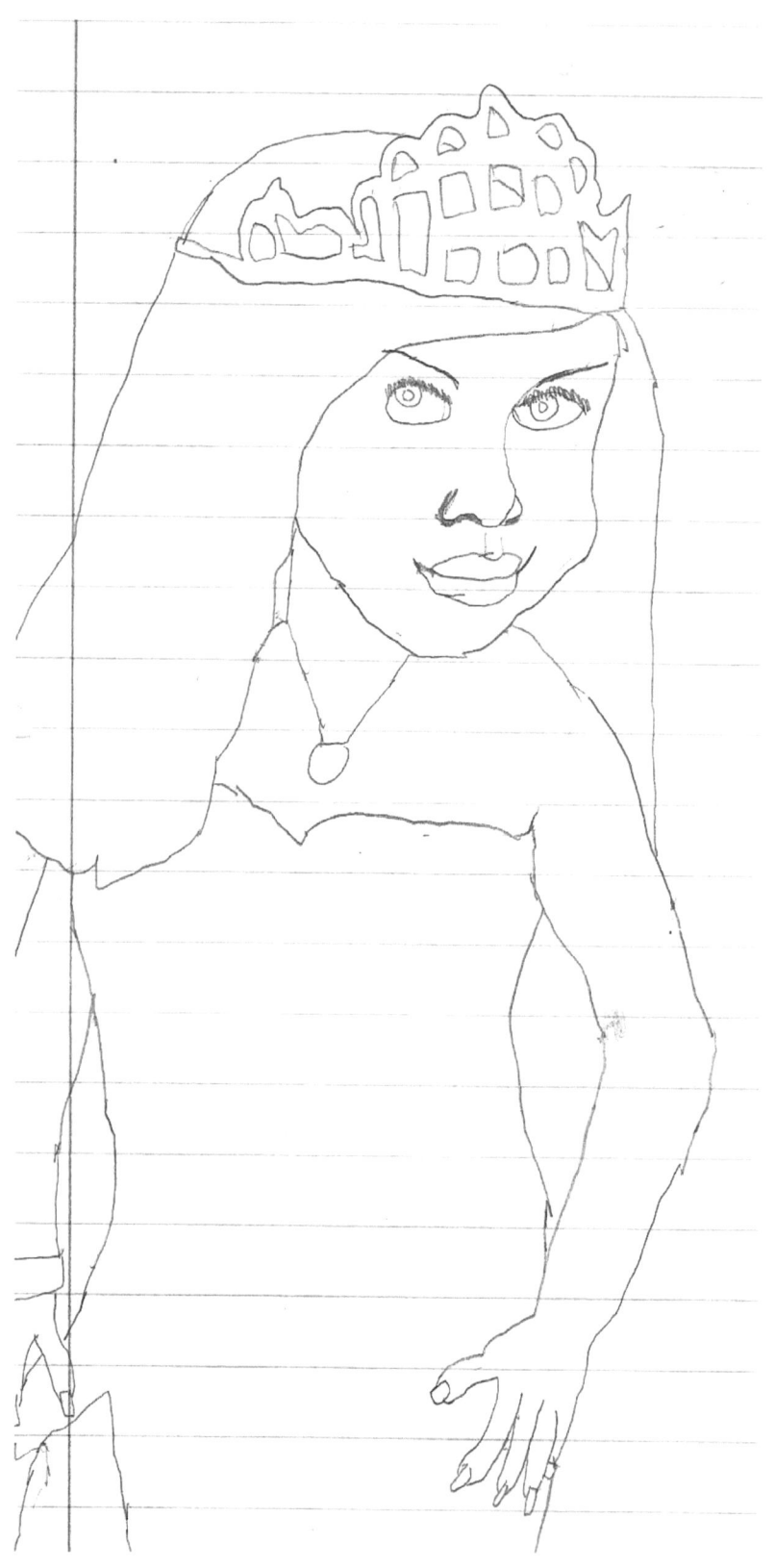

SQUIRREL DOODLES

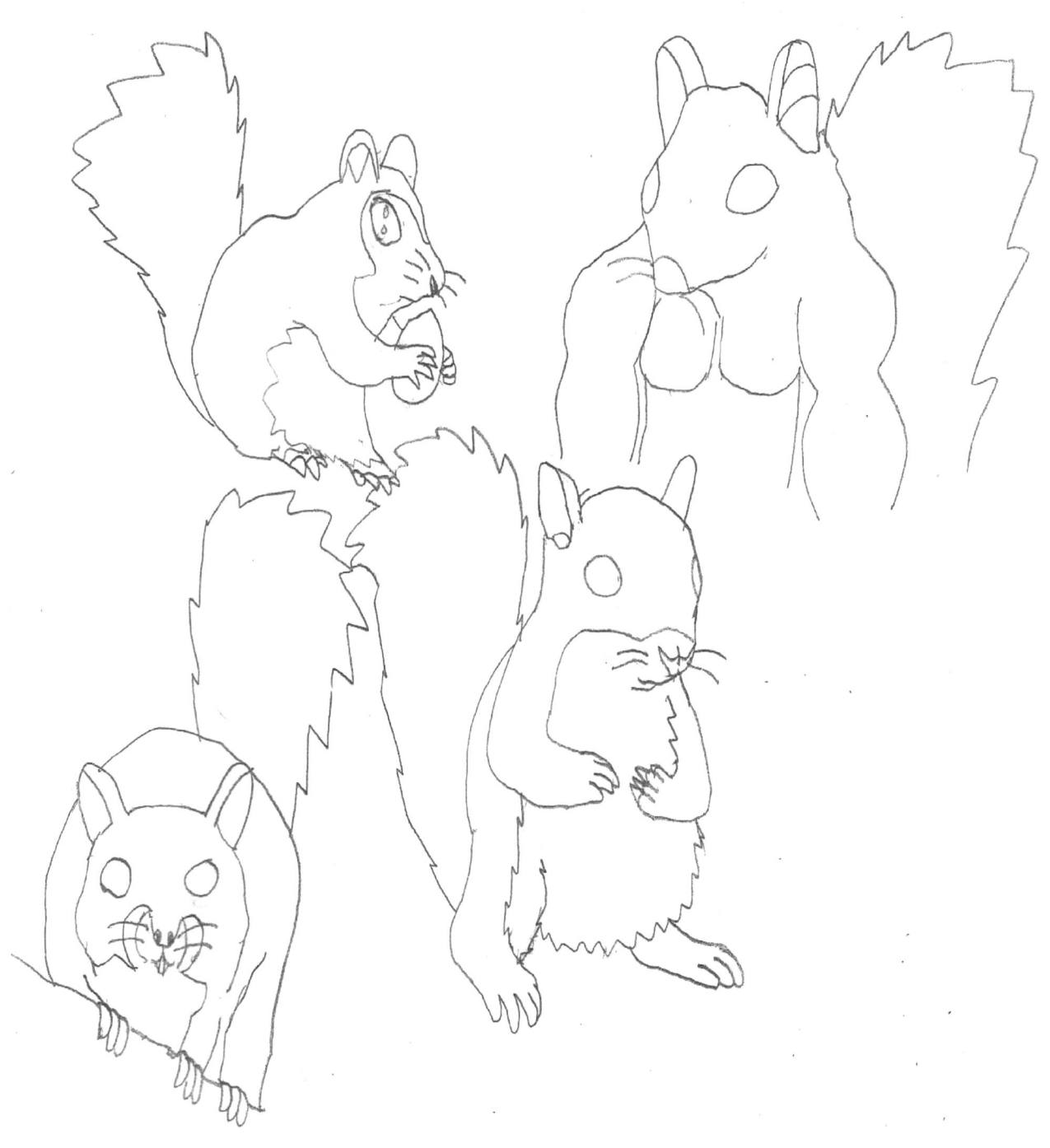

GABE'S WIFE, QUEEN TINA ANIMATED WEARING THE OUTFIT FROM A 2008 FASHION SHOW

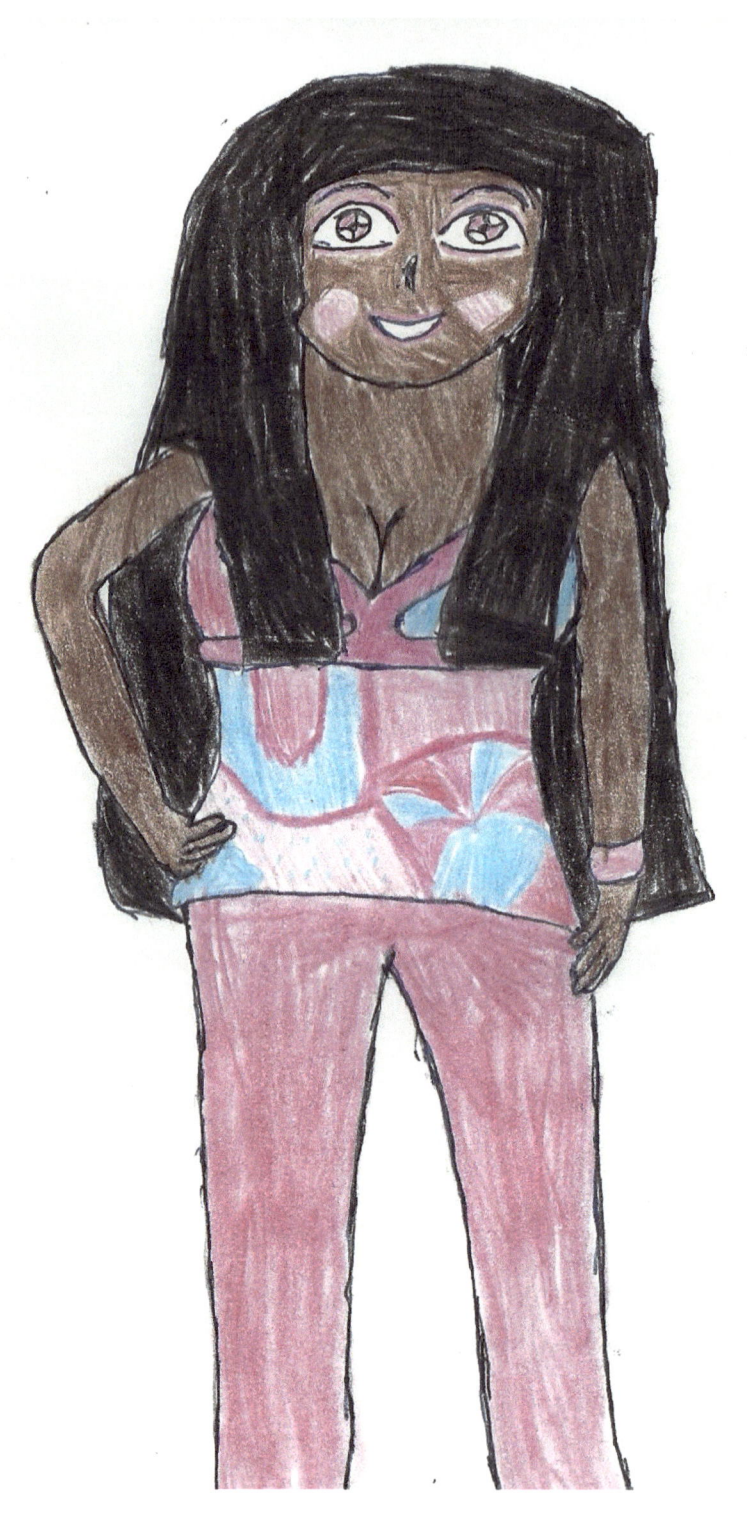

KING GABE AND QUEEN TINA ANIMATED ROYALTY

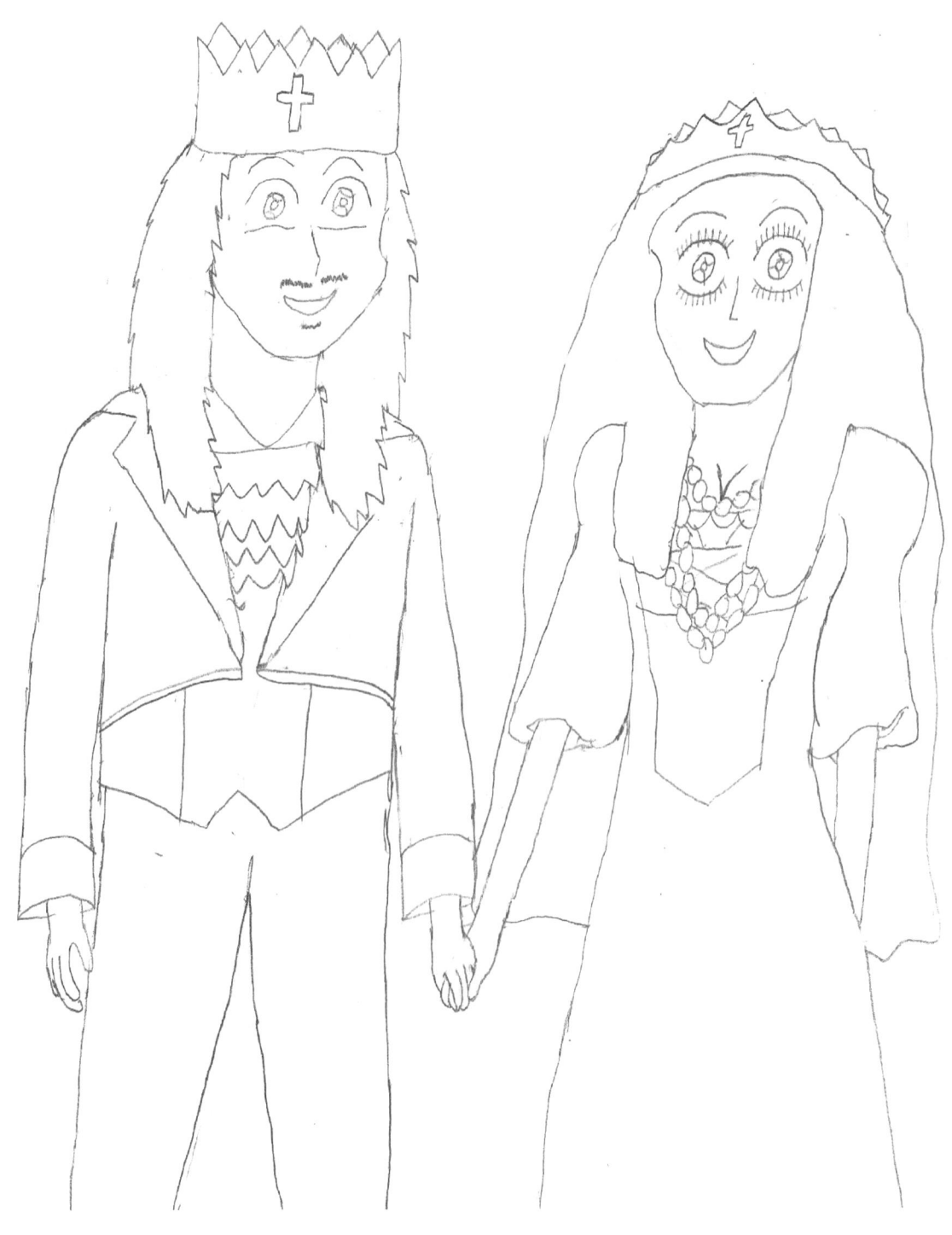

PROTOTYPE SAMUEL LEE PRINCETON/STAR STRIKER

BEFORE THE HEROES OF DREAMS BOOK SERIES IN 2011

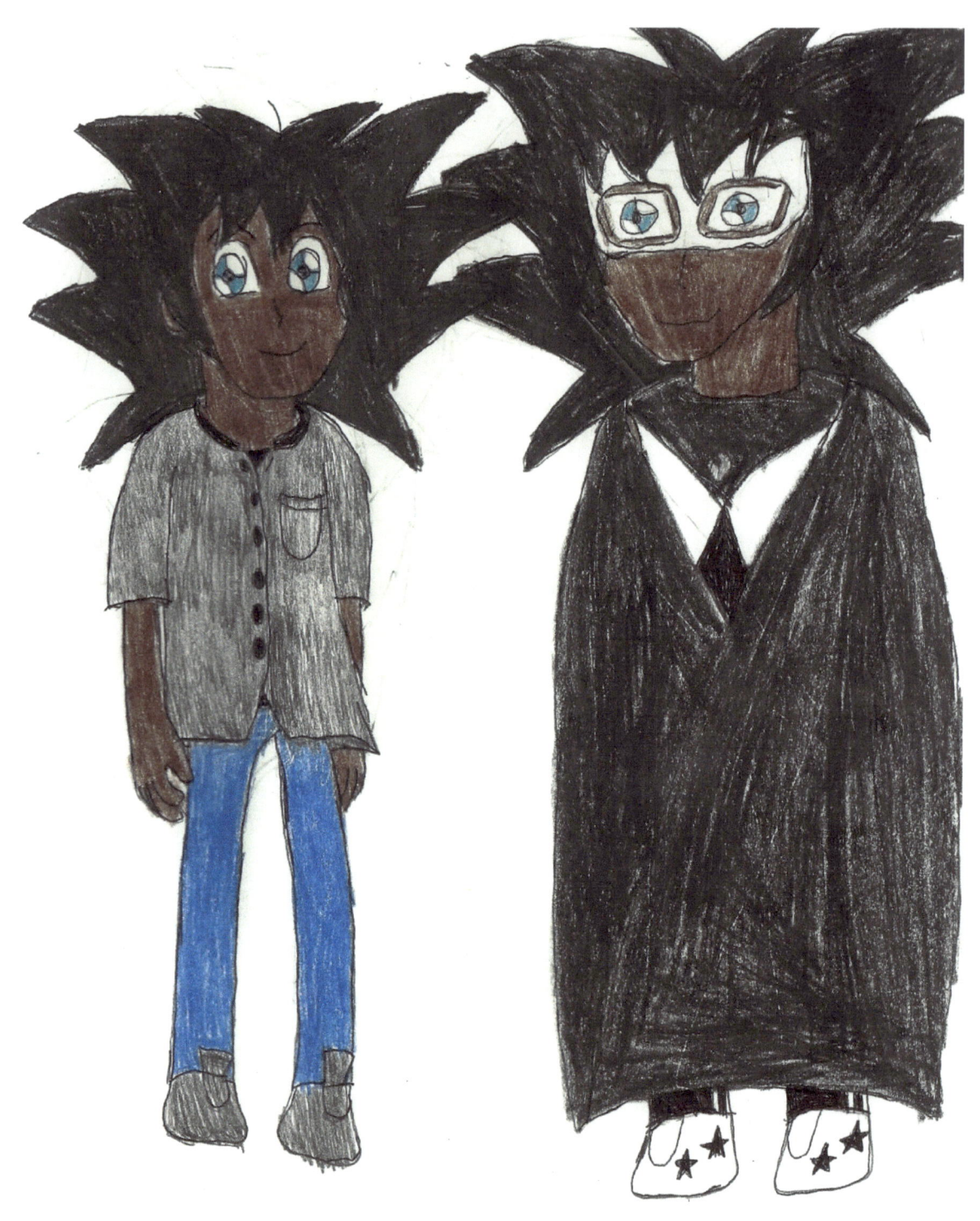

PROTOTYPE MELODY LEE SMITH/BUBBLELINA

BEFORE THE HEROES OF DREAMS BOOK SERIES IN 2011

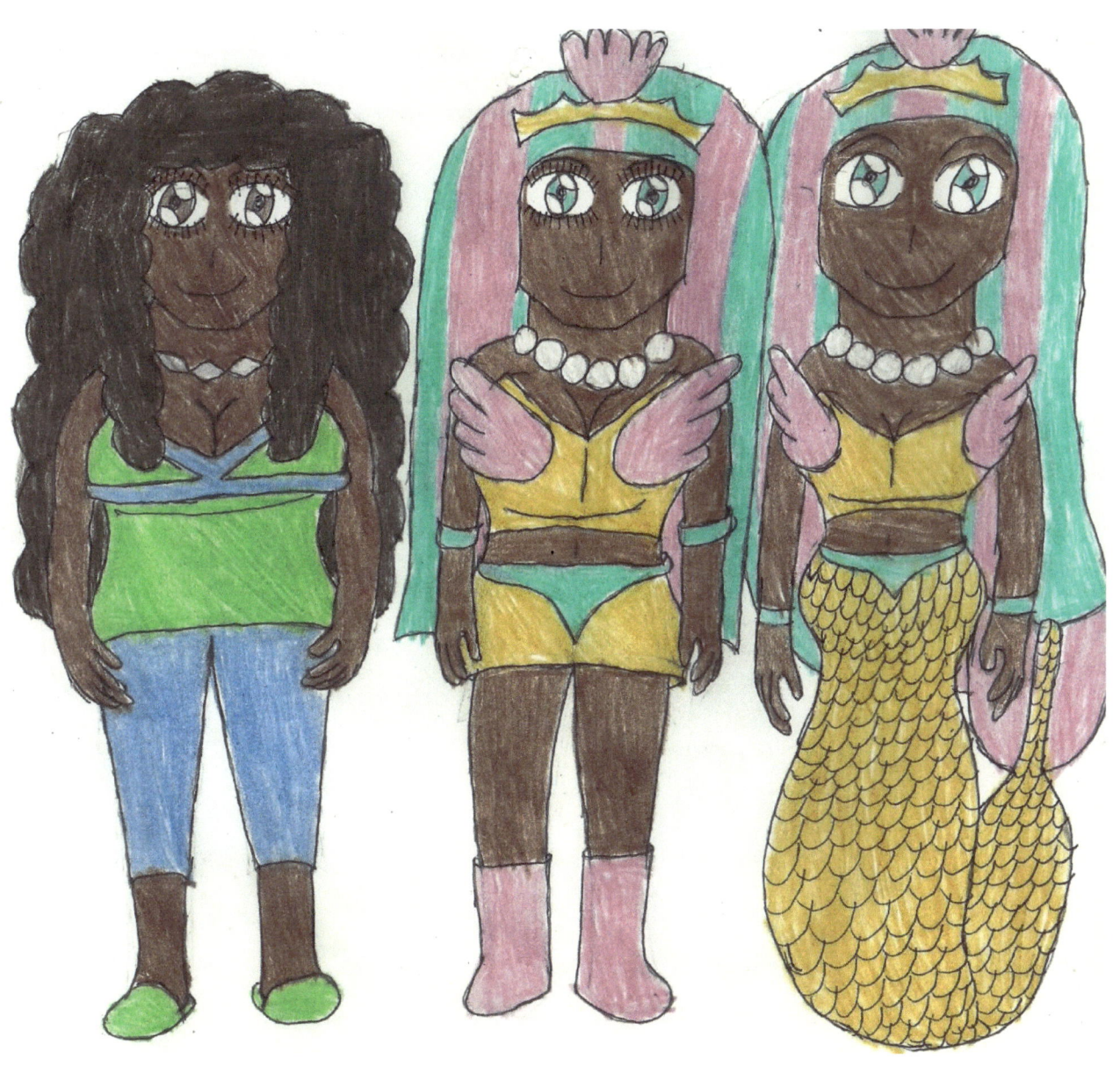

PROTOTYPE LEONARDO PRINCETON/AGENT LEE

BEFORE THE HEROES OF DREAMS BOOK SERIES IN 2011

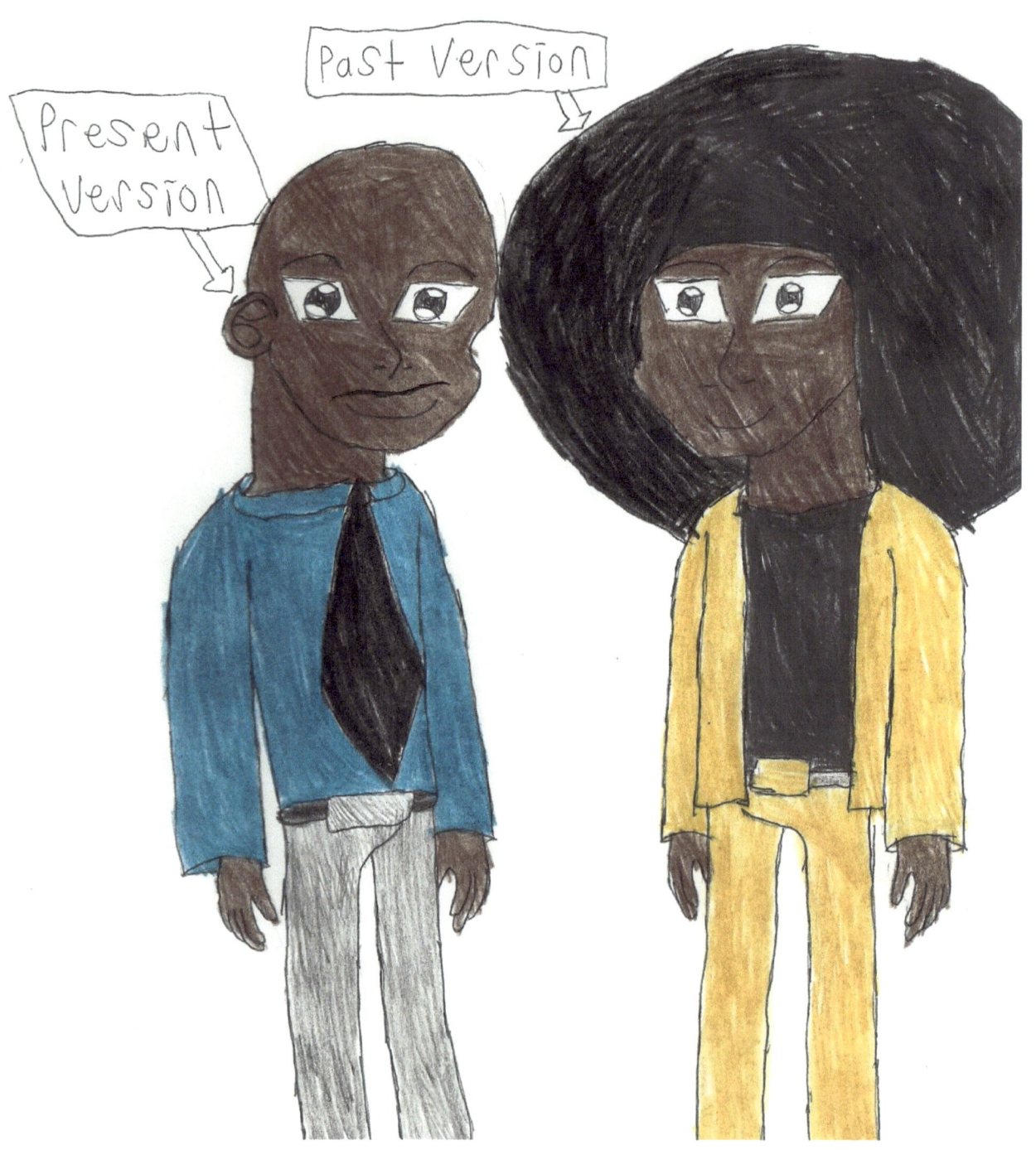

KING GABE AND QUEEN TINA AS KIDS WITH PUPPY LOVE

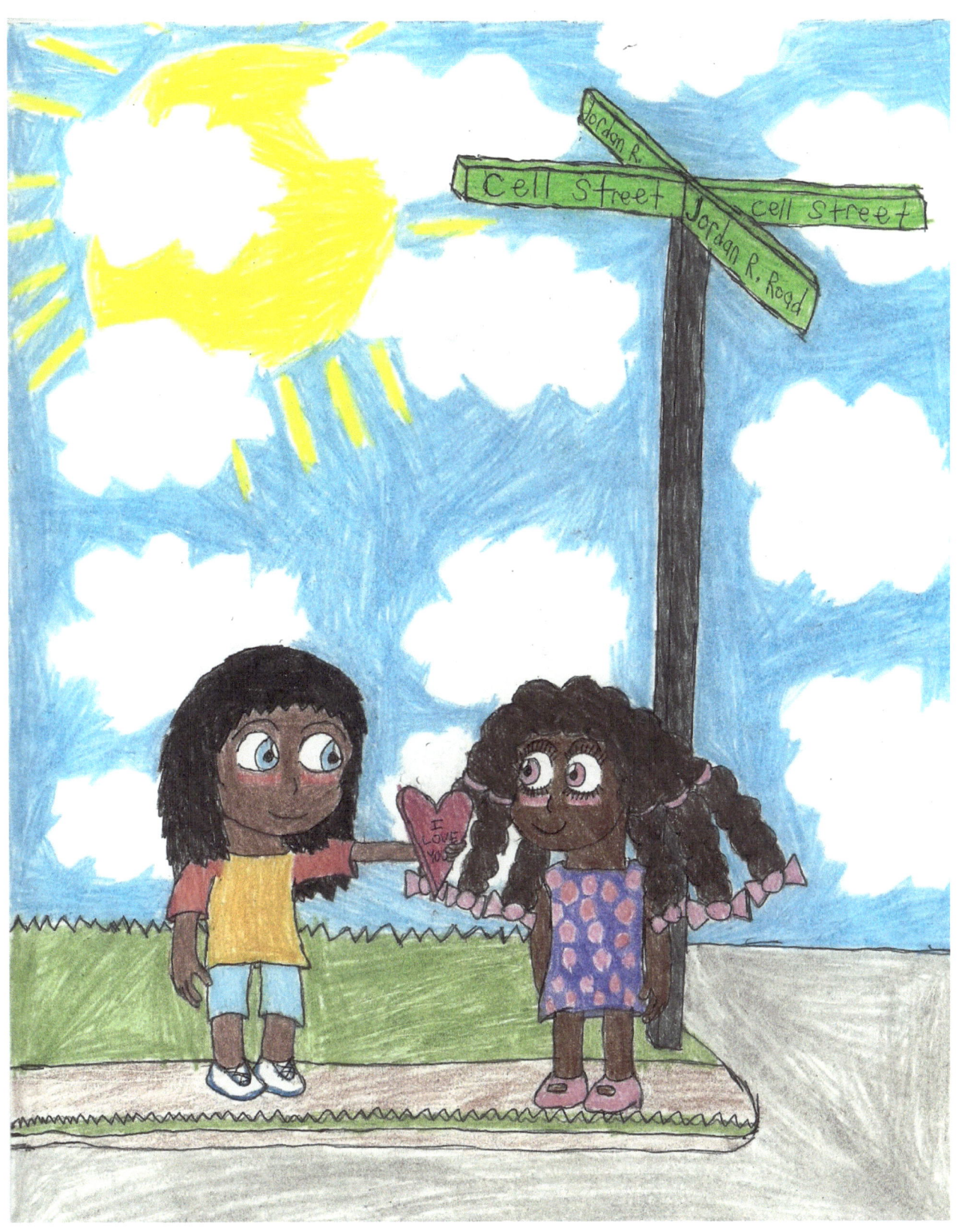

QUEEN TINA WITH JESUS CHRIST AFTER BAPTISM

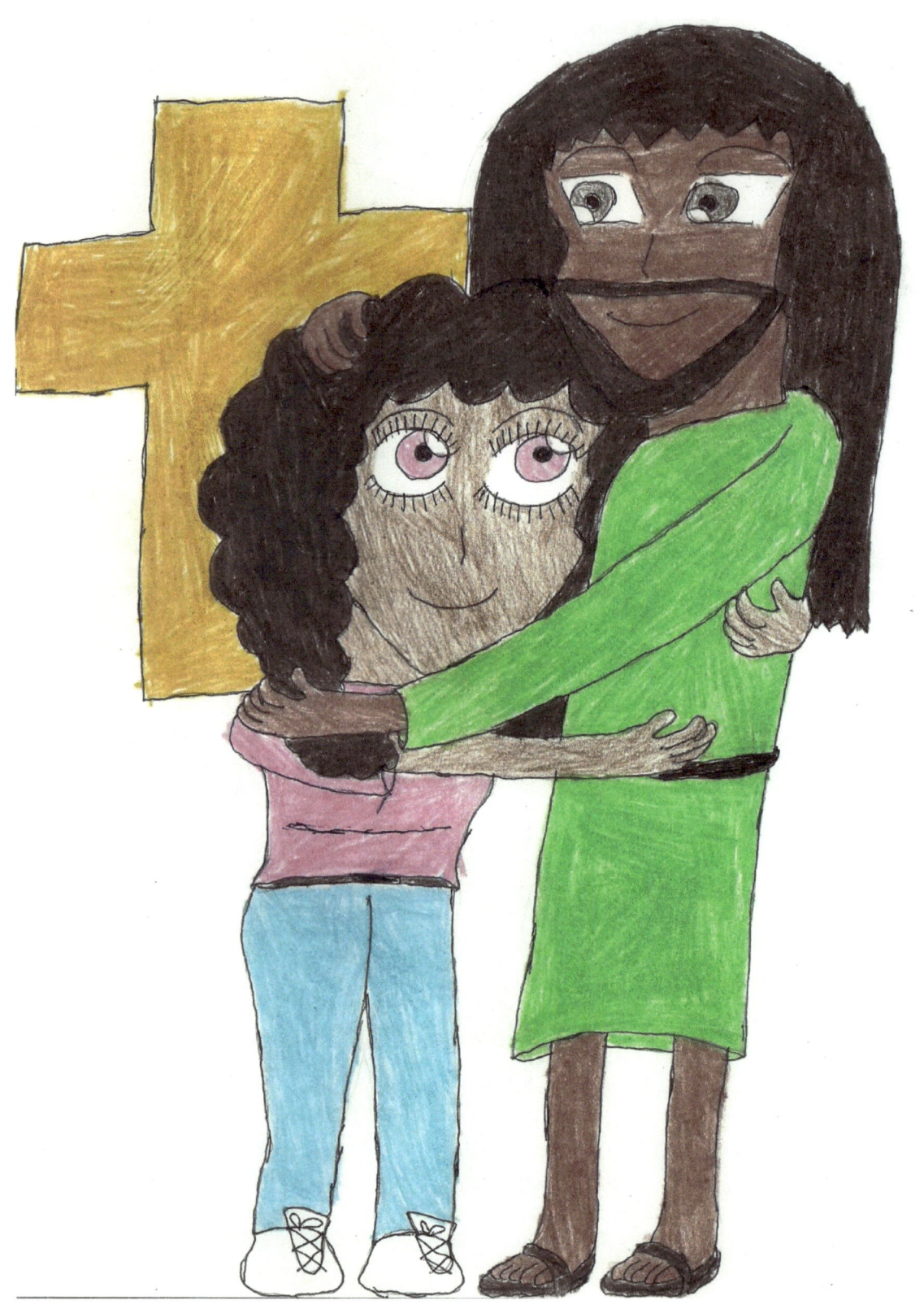

KING GABE WITH JESUS CHRIST AFTER BAPTISM

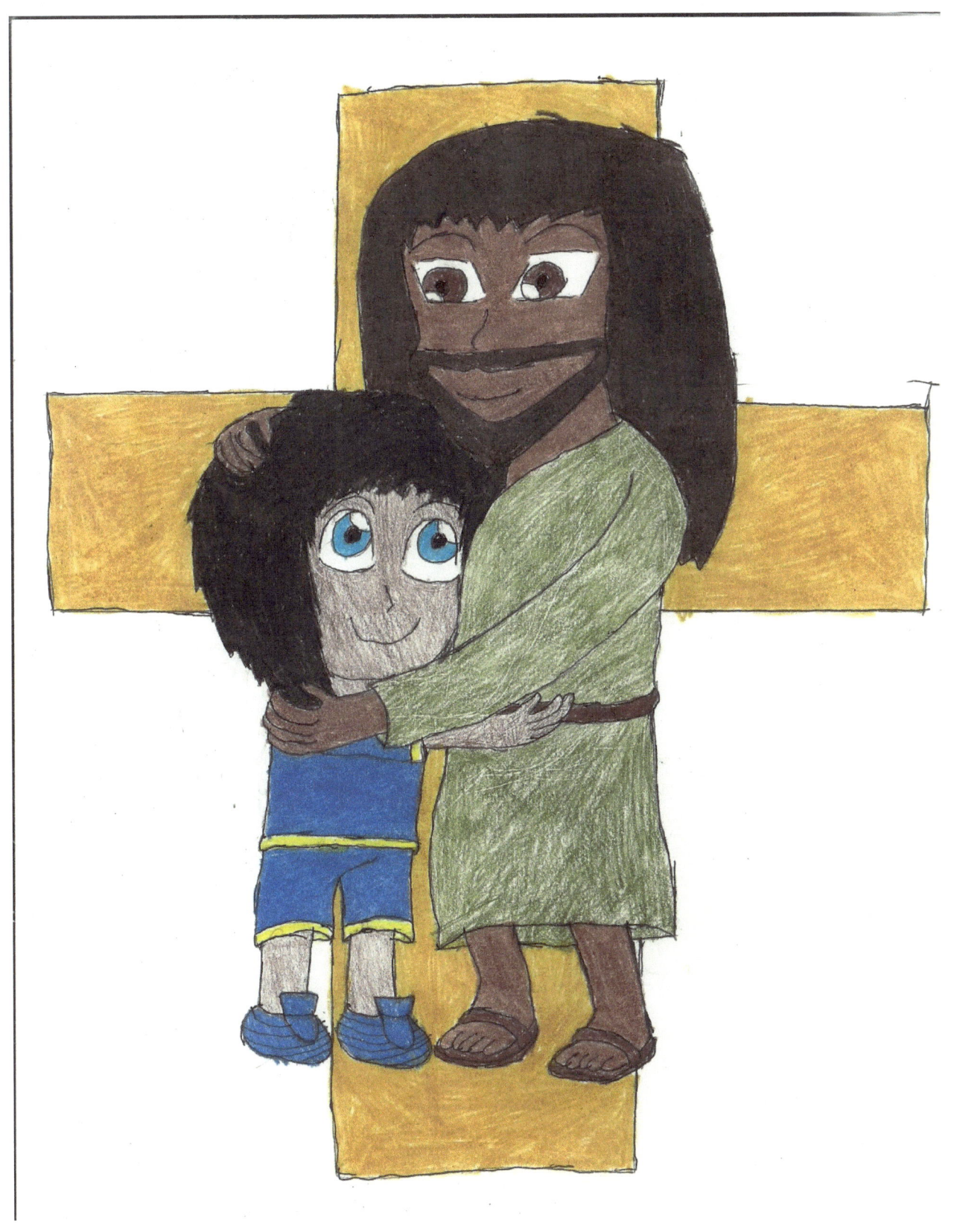

KING GABE AND QUEEN TINA'S FUTURE DREAM FAMILY

THE JOHNSONS

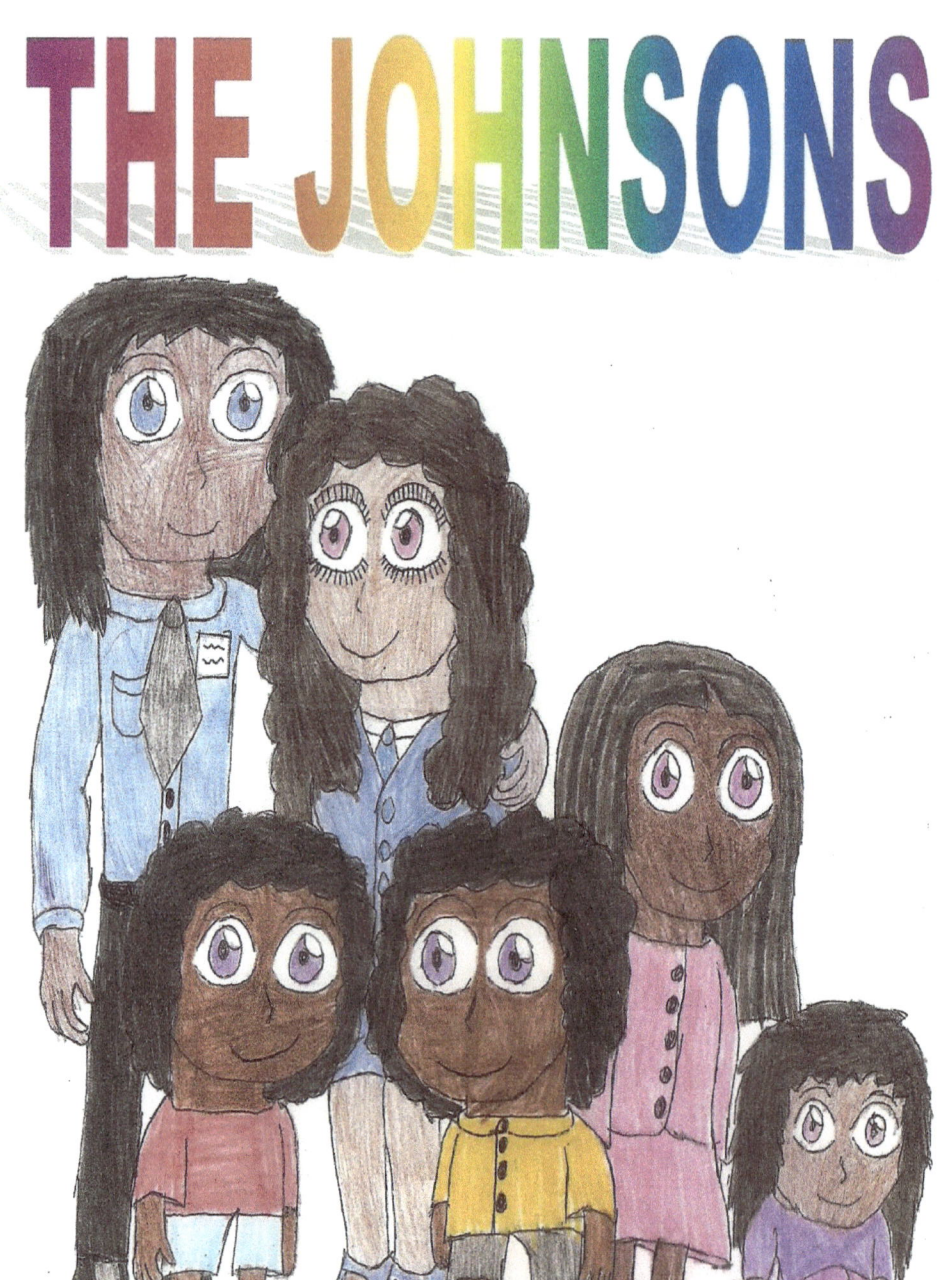

BROWNNY BEE BROWN

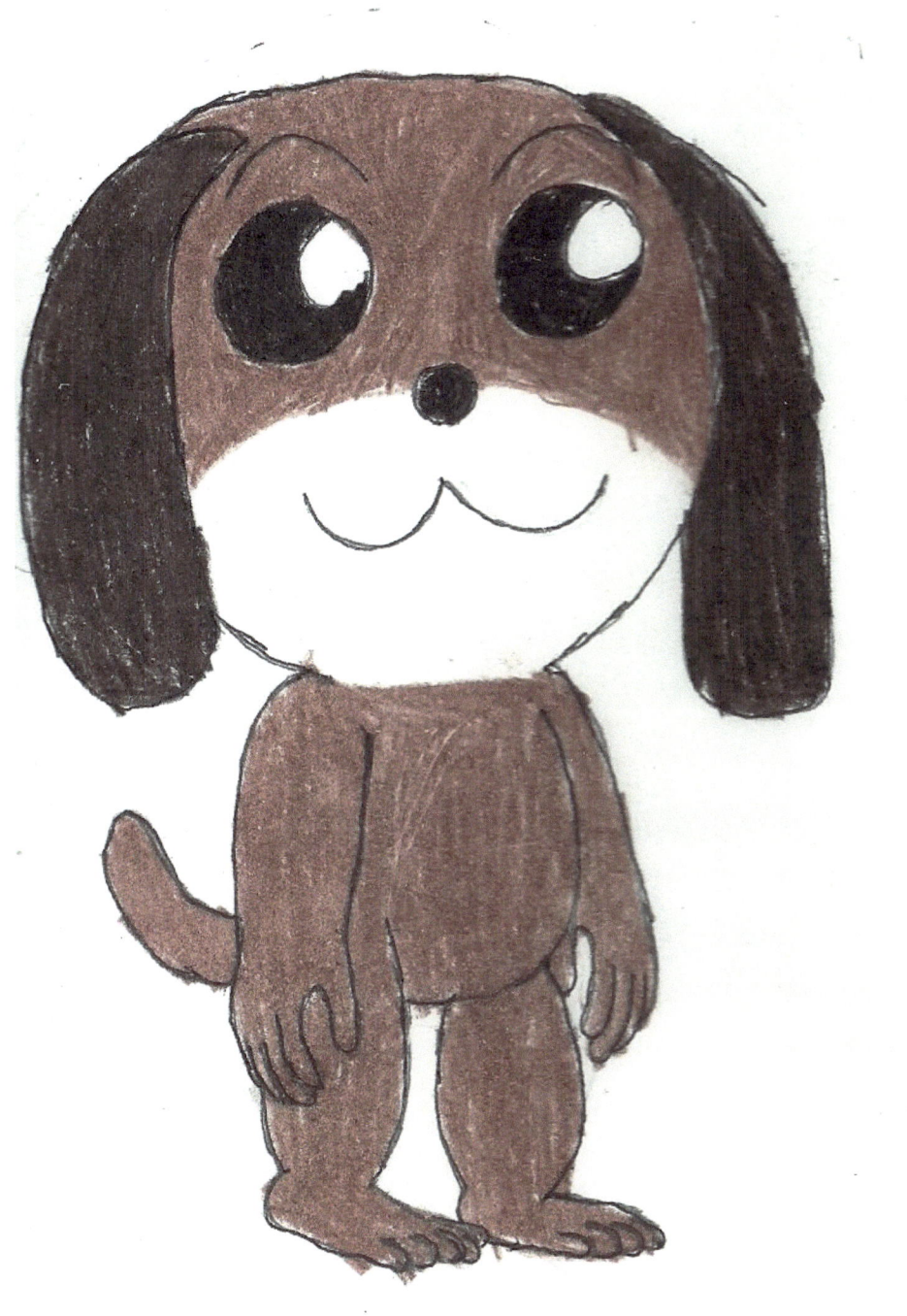

FELINA MAY KAT

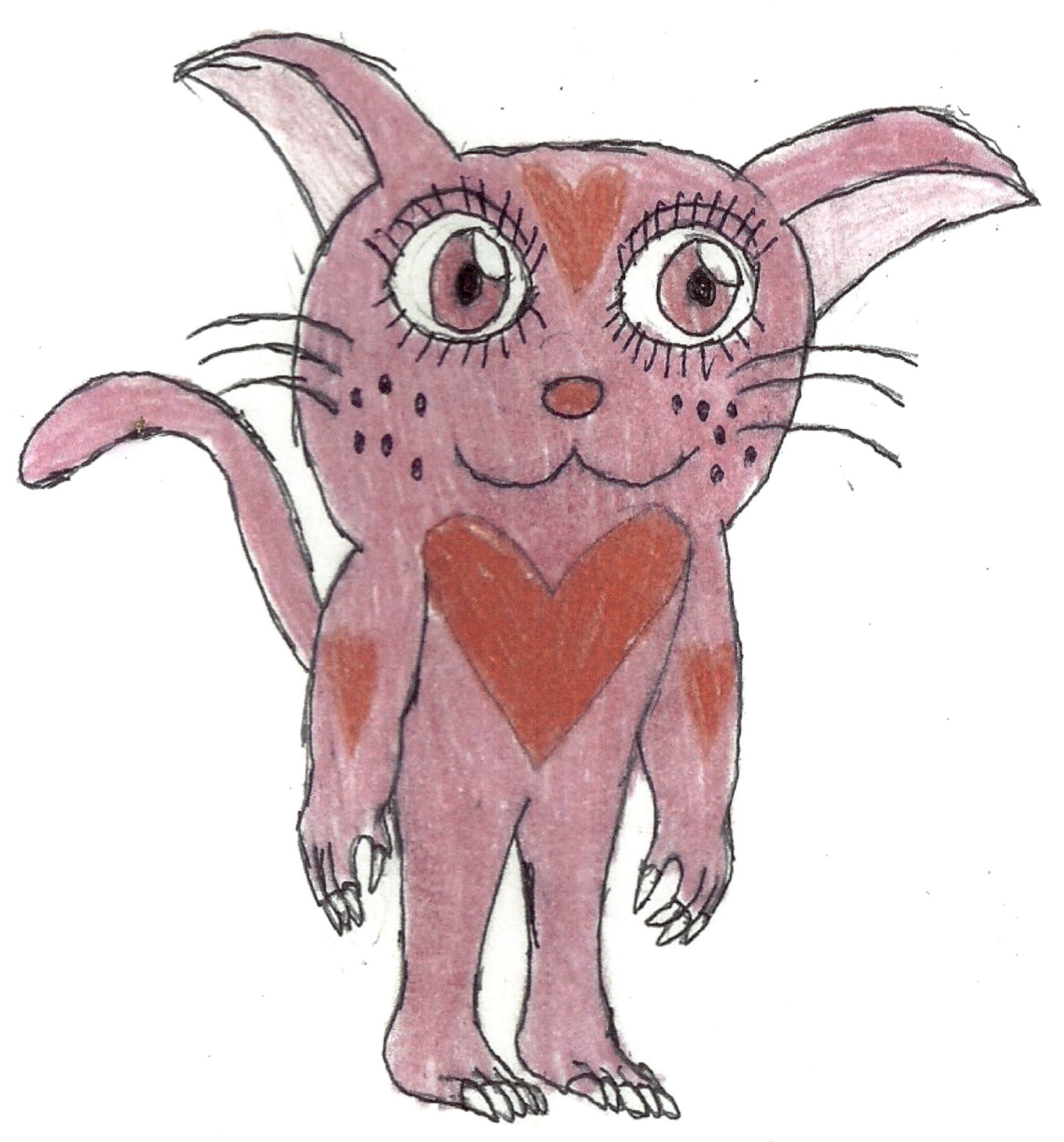

GABE PLAYING BASKETBALL WITH THE GUYS

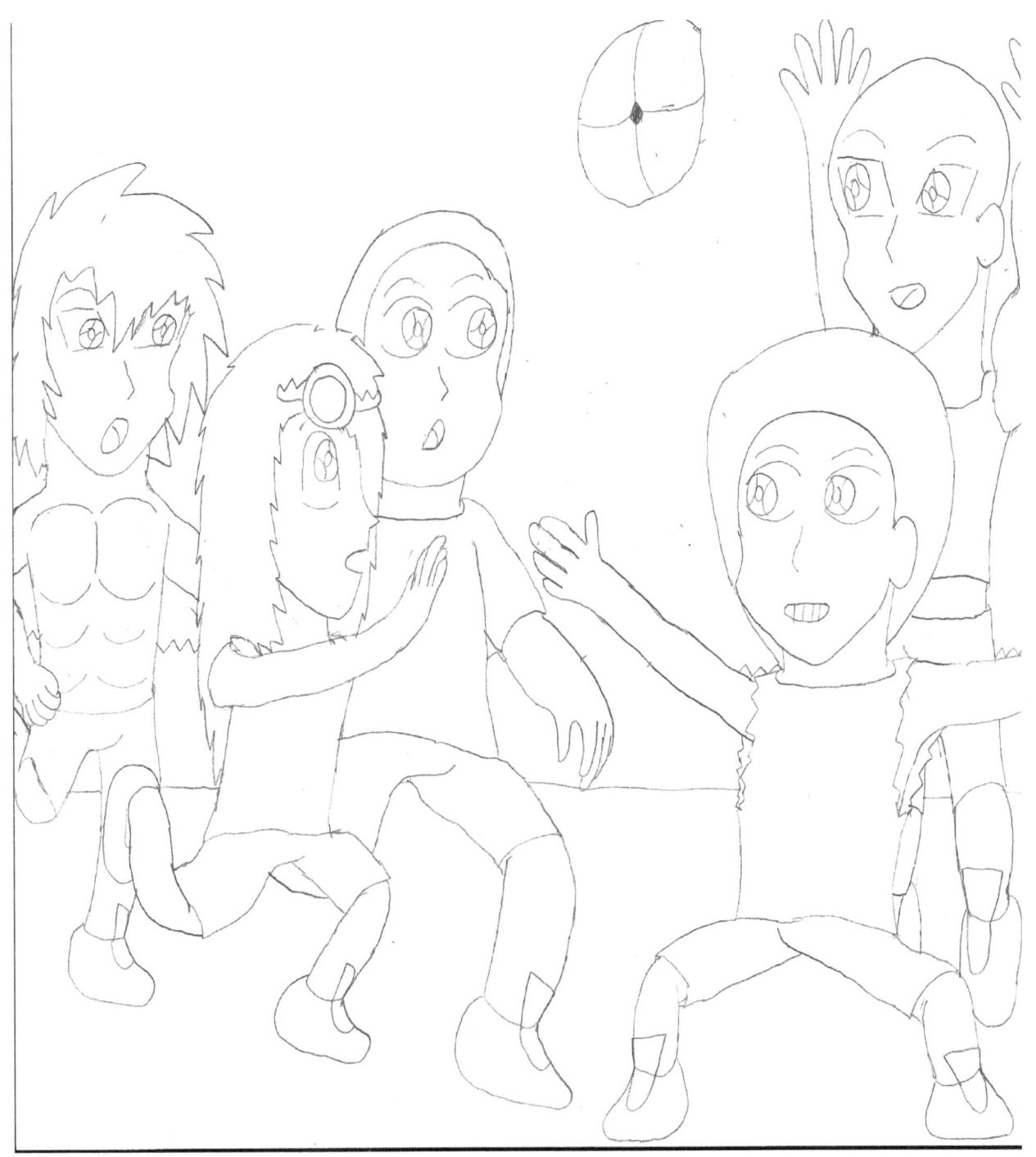

GABE'S IMAGINARY SISTER, TIYANA (A.K.A. TIKARI):

VERSION TWO

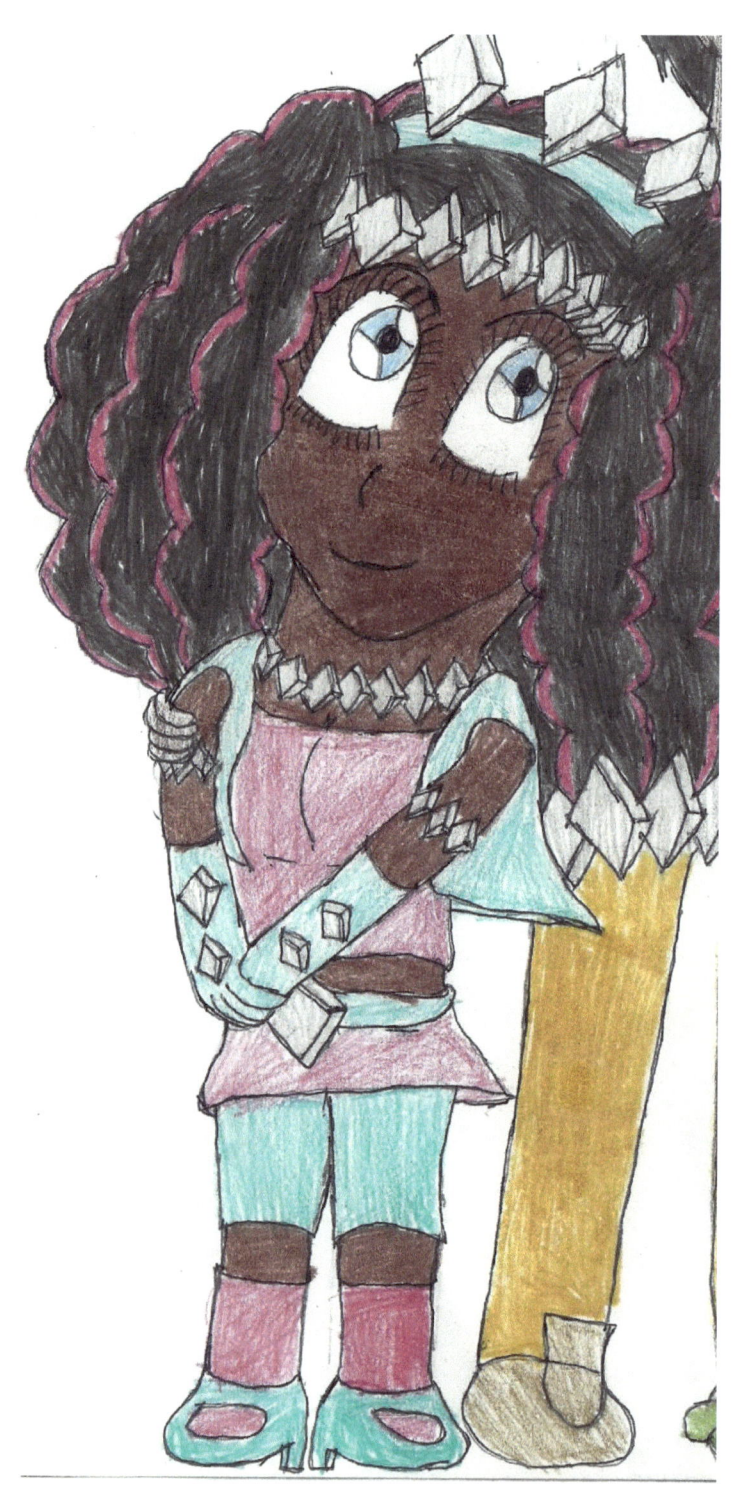

TIYANA AND HER FRIEND TY BACK TO SCHOOL SHOPPING

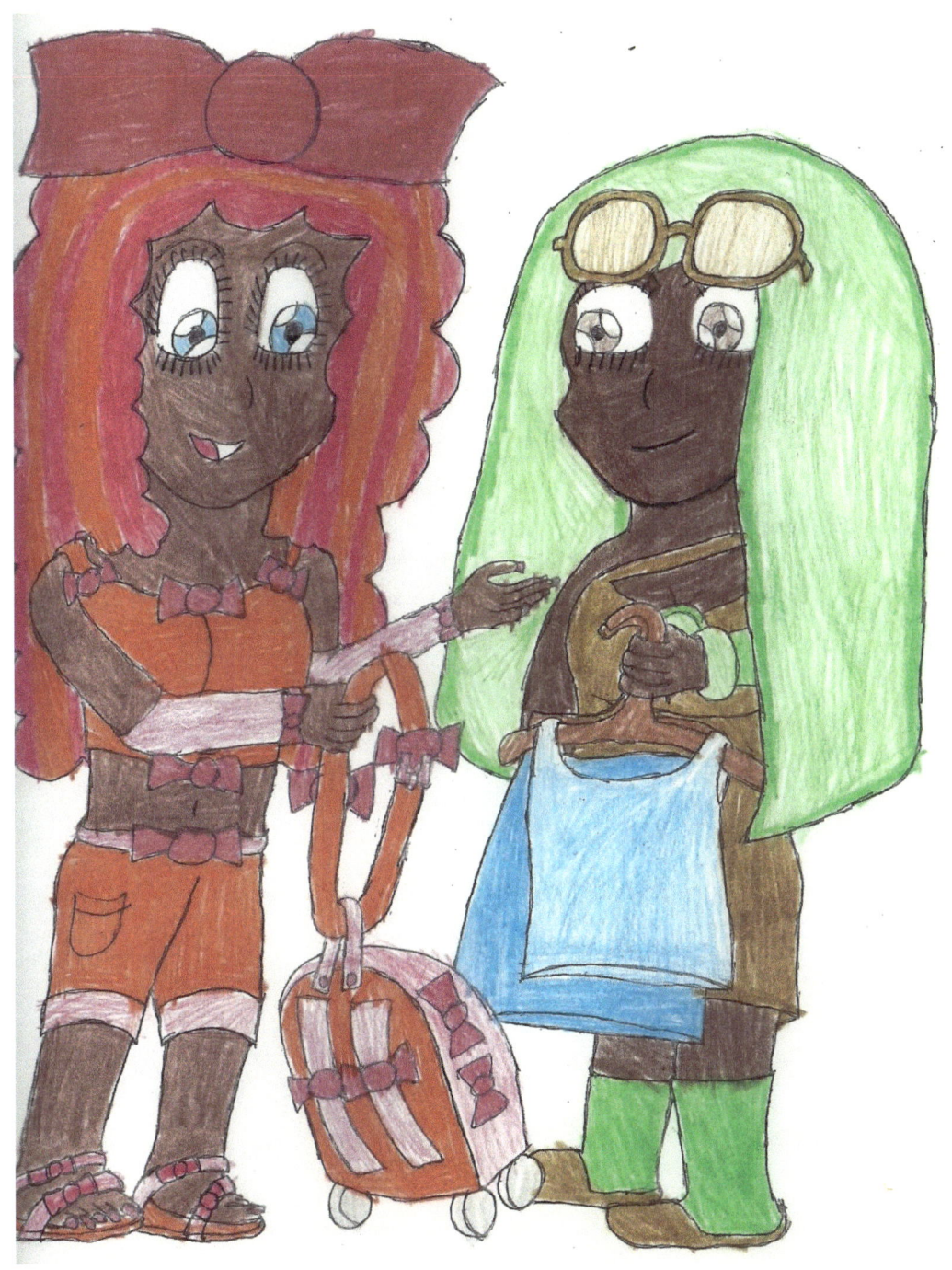

DARKINA, THE DARK HARPY: VERSION ONE

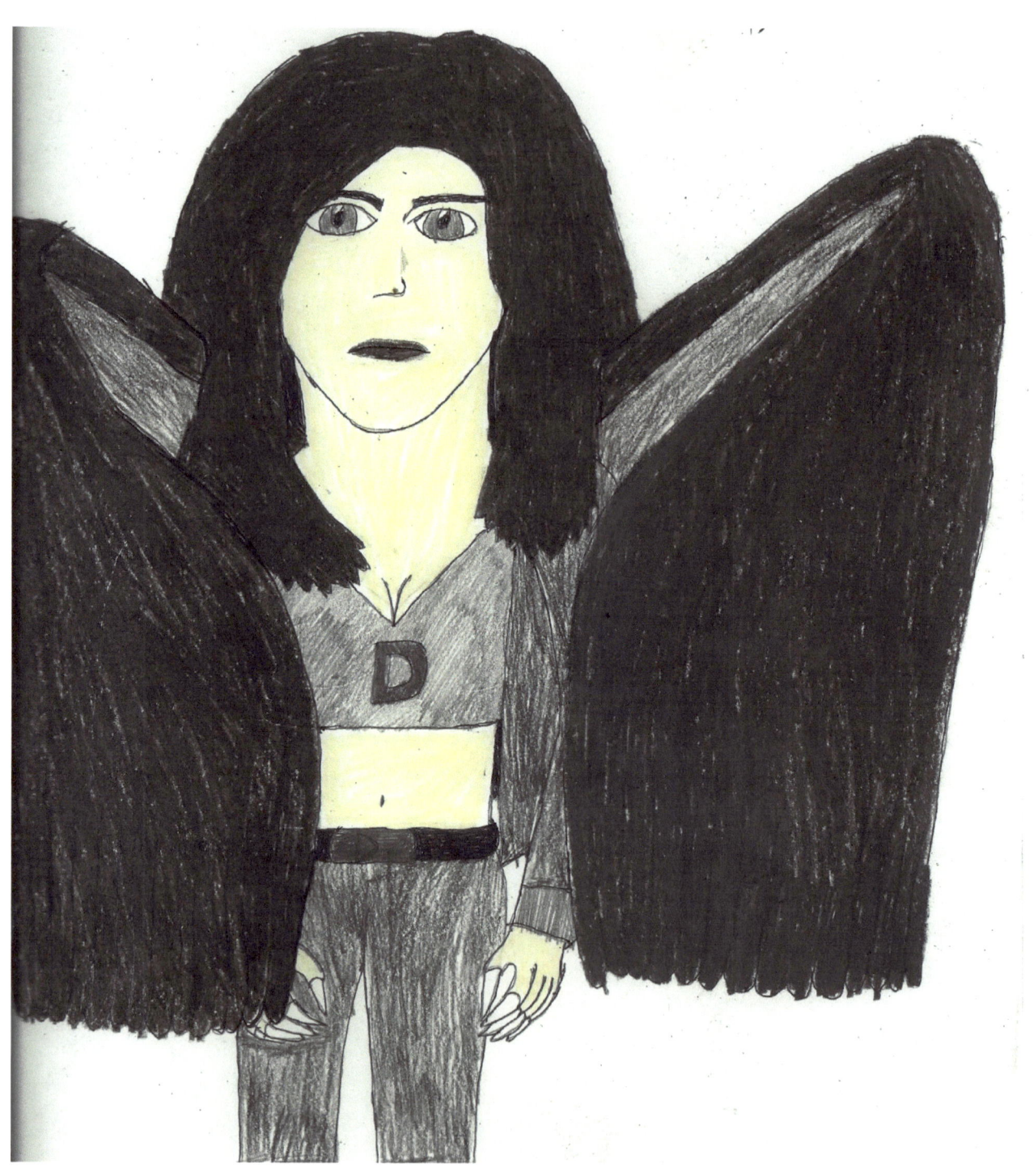

DARKINA, THE DARK HARPY: VERSION TWO

(ALONG WITH HER HUMAN FORM, SHANICE)

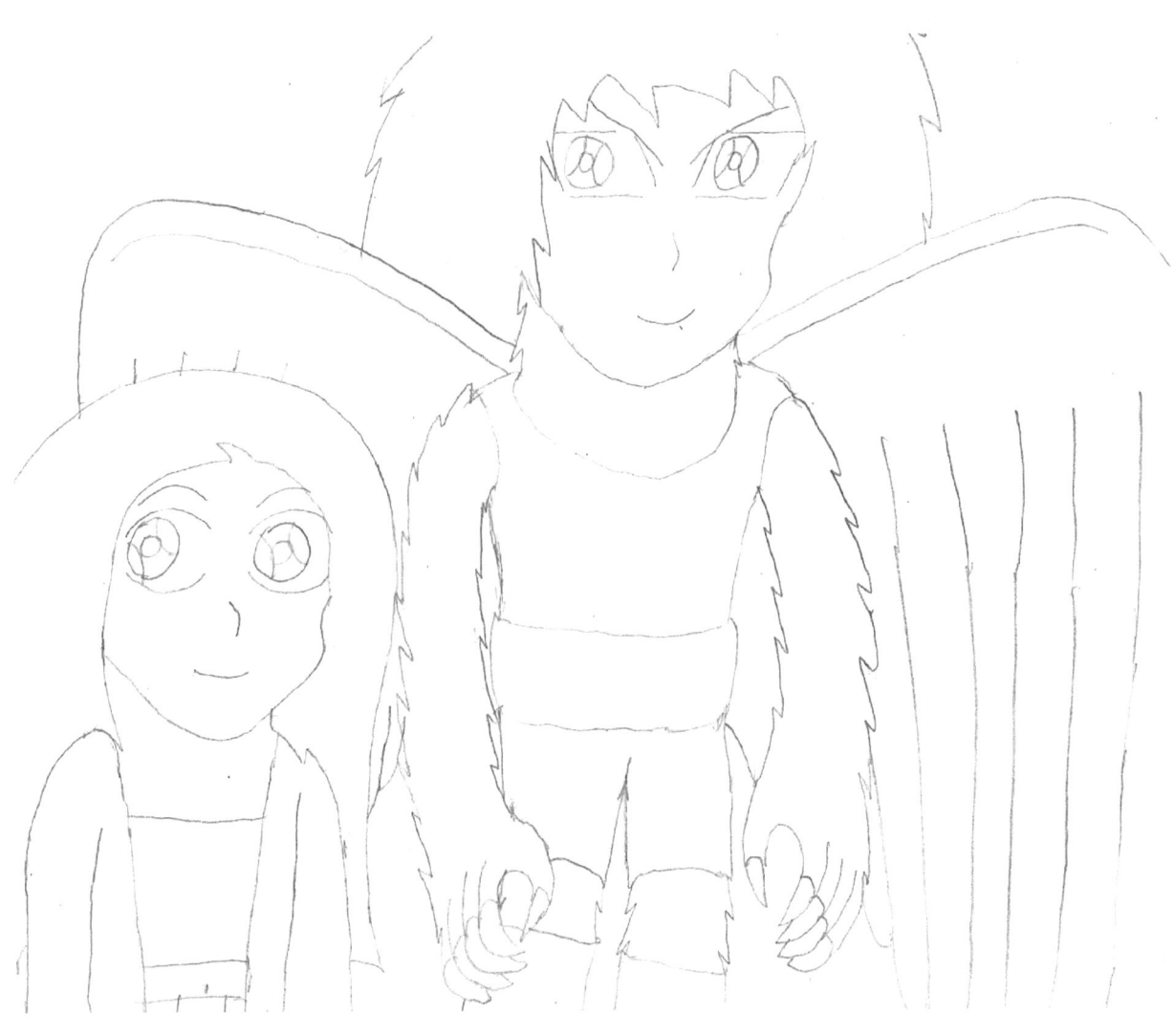

CHECK OUT THESE OTHER BOOKS BY THE AUTHOR!

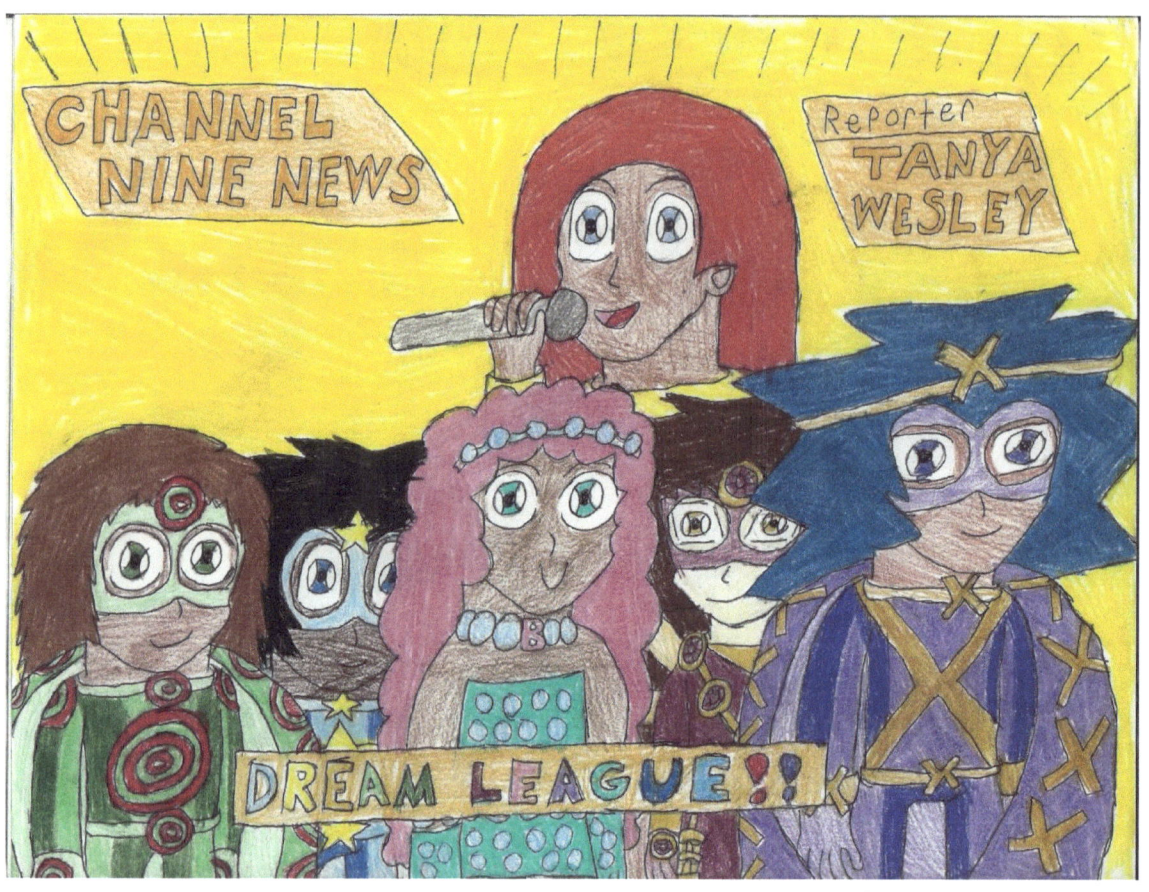

HEROES OF DREAMS THE SERIES

VOLUME ONE: "A HEROIC DREAM BEGINS"

VOLUME TWO: "RIGHT ON TARGET"

VOLUME THREE: "MIND OF THE SWORDS OF HONOR"

VOLUME FOUR: "DISCOVERY WITHIN THE BUBBLES"

VOLUME FIVE: "THE MYSTERIOUS MIRACLES OF SALVATION"

FOR MORE INFORMATION ON HOW TO GET THESE BOOKS, SEND AN EMAIL TO
MEGAGABE@GMAIL.COM OR CALL (318)422-6203

ALSO BE SURE TO VISIT WWW.HEROESOFDREAMSTHESERIES.COM

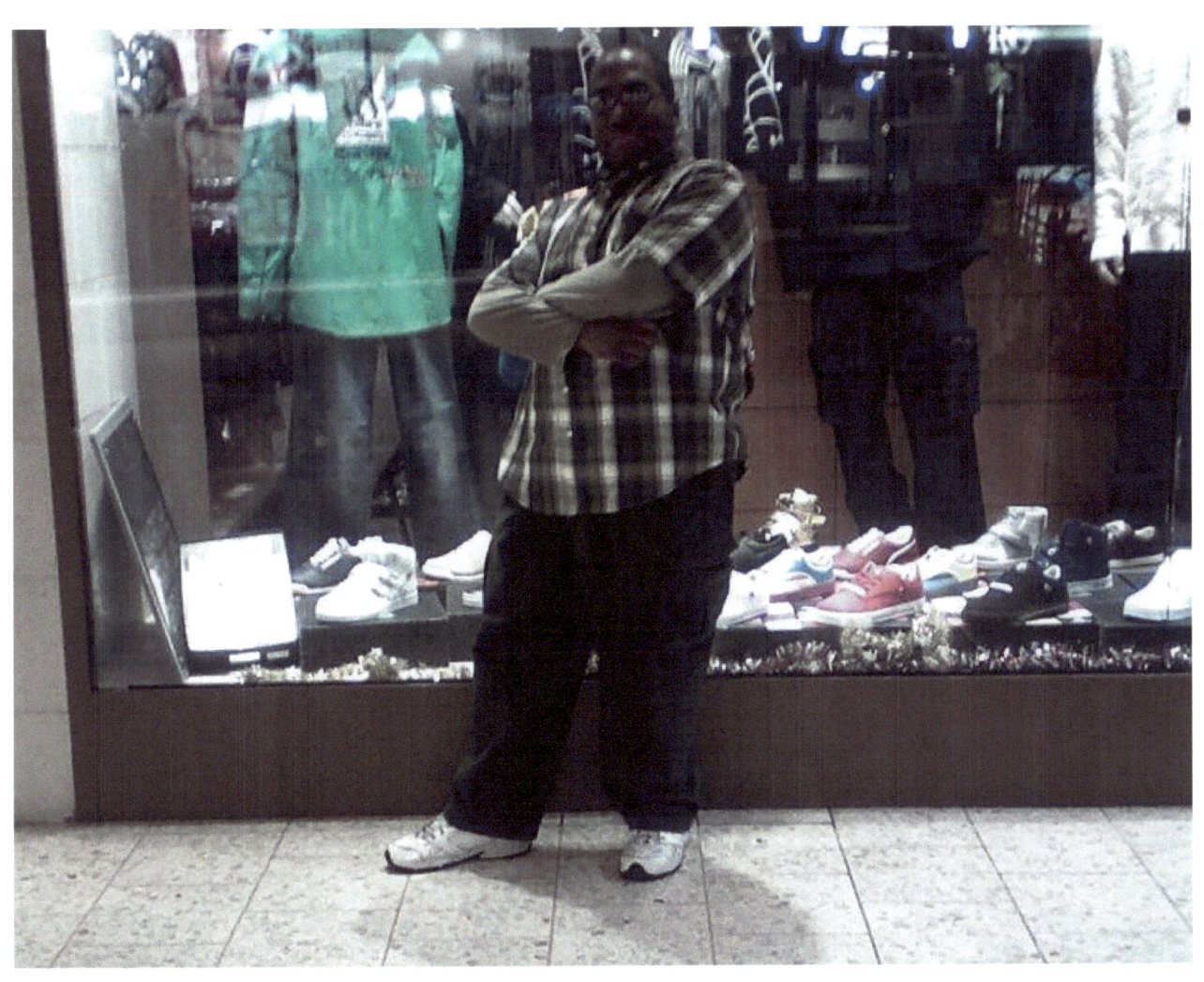

MORE TO COME IN KING GABE'S WORLD

AND IN HEROES OF DREAMS THE SERIES!

www.ingramcontent.com/pod-product-compliance
Lightning Source LLC
Chambersburg PA
CBHW041300180526
45172CB00003B/916